Studies on the
Foundation Stone Meditation

STUDIES ON THE
FOUNDATION STONE
MEDITATION

Valentin Tomberg

Introductions by
Robert Powell & George Adams

Translated by
R. H. Bruce

Revised by
James Wetmore

LOGO SOPHIA
San Rafael CA

First published in the USA
by LogoSophia Press
an imprint of Sophia Perennis
© Robert Powell 2010

Series editor: James R. Wetmore

For information, address:
LogoSophia Press, P.O. Box 151011
San Rafael, CA 94915

Library of Congress Cataloging-in-Publication Data

Tomberg, Valentin.
[Einige Ergebnisse der Arbeit an der Grundsteinmeditation
Rudolf Steiners. English]
Studies on the Foundation stone meditation / Valentin Tomberg;
introduction by Robert Powell & George Adams;
translated by R. H. Bruce; revised by James Wetmore.

p. cm.
"The Foundation stone meditation"—P.
Includes bibliographical references.
ISBN 978 1 59731 503 6 (pbk.: alk. paper)
1. Steiner, Rudolf, 1861–1925. Grundsteinmeditation. 2. Meditation—
Anthroposophy. I. Wetmore, James. II. Steiner, Rudolf, 1861–1925.
Grundsteinmeditation. English. III. Title.
BP595.S894G793813 2010
299'.935—dc22   2010012817

CONTENTS

INTRODUCTION

ROBERT POWELL

THE TEXT of the Foundation Stone meditation follows this introduction to Valentin Tomberg's *Studies on The Foundation Stone Meditation*. This text was first spoken by Rudolf Steiner on Christmas Day 1923 as a meditation enfolding a supersensible reality that has been called by various names: the Holy Grail and the Philosophers' Stone being two of the more traditional designations for what Rudolf Steiner called the *Foundation Stone of Love*. He indicates that through living deeply and intensively with this meditation one is able to receive the *Foundation Stone of Love* into one's heart.

This meditation was given at a special moment in time, at the onset of the Second Coming of Christ. The first three verses of the Foundation Stone meditation are *addressed to the human soul by Christ* at this time of His return in a supersensible form in the world of life forces, the ethereal realm. It is in an ethereal form and as a moral force in Nature—'*in the clouds*', '*like lightning flashing from the east and shining in the west*'—that He is manifesting Himself now at this time of His Second Coming.

The Foundation Stone meditation is a powerful source of attunement to this new manifestation of Christ. It encapsulates the event corresponding in our time to the Baptism in the River Jordan two thousand years ago. At that time John the Baptist spoke the words, '*Behold the Lamb of God*'—indicating Christ (the Lamb) incarnating into the human being of Jesus of Nazareth as a Presence on the physical level of our planet Earth. Now, in our time, the laying of the *Foundation Stone of Love* through Rudolf Steiner is an expression of the baptismal event of Christ's Second Coming, heralding His Presence in the ethereal realm enveloping and permeating Mother Earth. Through the *Foundation Stone of Love* one is 'baptized' into the Second Coming of Christ. Rudolf Steiner, as the human being through whom this meditation was given to humanity, had the role of a modern-day 'John the Baptist', as the one whose task it was to herald the coming of Christ in the ethereal realm.

The first three verses of the Foundation Stone meditation—addressed to the human soul by Christ—each begin with the words *Human Soul*! The fourth verse is an answer—or echo—from the human being, as a prayer to Christ in His supersensible form, in response to the first three verses.

The first verse addresses the human will, indicating that through the activity of *spirit recollection* the human being can attain to true gnosis. Knowledge as to how the human being '*comes to being in God's I*' has always been the goal of gnosis—knowing the Divine. The second verse addresses the realm of human feeling, indicating that through the activity of *spirit awareness*, where the heart becomes the directing center of consciousness, the human being can attain to true mysticism or '*union with the World I*'. The third verse addresses the human thought life, indicating that through the activity of *spirit beholding* the human being can attain to free will, recalling that in Christ's teaching the true goal of attainment of free will is to *serve the Divine* in the sense of the words, '*Not my will, but thy will be done.*' Through beholding in the spirit, the '*eternal aims of Gods*'—the beings of the celestial hierarchies—are revealed; and there is no greater calling than to serve these eternal aims by way of actively participating in bringing the future to realization. Lastly, the fourth verse refers to the Mystery of Golgotha as evolution's turning point of time through the birth of the true 'I'—bestowed upon humanity through the coming of Christ two thousand years ago. The fourth verse culminates in a prayer offered to Christ in His supersensible form, a prayer that is highly appropriate for our time.

The structure and content of the Foundation Stone meditation reveal the essence of Christ's gift to humanity at this time of the Second Coming—bestowing an impulse elevating the human soul to an awareness of a living relationship with the Eternal Trinity and with the nine levels of celestial hierarchies weaving in the whole of creation in service of the Godhead:

Angels (Guardian Spirits of individuals)—*Moon* sphere
Archangels (Guardian Spirits of peoples)—*Mercury* sphere
Archai (Guardian Spirits of epochs of time)—*Venus* sphere
Exusiai (Elohim, Powers, Spirits of Form)—*Sun* sphere
Dynamis (Mights, Virtues, Spirits of Movement)—*Sun* sphere
Kyriotetes (Dominions, Lords, Spirits of Wisdom)—*Sun* sphere
Thrones (Spirits of Will, Beings of the Word)—*Mars* sphere
Cherubim (Spirits of Wisdom and Harmony)—*Jupiter* sphere
Seraphim (Spirits of Love, Beings of Memory)—*Saturn* sphere

Working with the Foundation Stone meditation is a powerful individual practice, which leads to a deep and profound experience of the *Foundation Stone of Love*. In this sense it is a fulfillment of the *'hidden knowledge of the Grail'* spoken of by Rudolf Steiner in his book *An Outline of Esoteric Science*:

> *The Mystery of Christ will permeate human beings' thinking, their feeling, and their will—ever increasingly as time goes on. The 'hidden knowledge of the Grail' will become manifest and grow to be a power in humanity's life, entering ever more fully into all the ways and walks of human beings.*

ROBERT POWELL

INTRODUCTION

GEORGE ADAMS

The following text preceding Parts One and Two of Valentin Tomberg's *Studies on The Foundation Stone Meditation* was written by George Adams as an introduction to the first English translation of this work, published in 1936 by the Anthroposophical Society in Great Britain. It has been edited for the present 2010 edition.

STUDENTS of Rudolf Steiner have been greatly helped by Valentin Tomberg's studies on the Old and the New Testaments, excellent translations of which are available.[1] We are now able to add a translation of the Russian-Estonian author's work upon another and very central theme, namely the Foundation Stone Meditation given by Rudolf Steiner at Christmas 1923.

While adding a word of welcome and of gratitude both to author and translator, I have a special reason for writing a brief introduction, namely the difficulties, both for translator and reader, arising from the fact that the meditation verses themselves, which form the basis of this study, first had to be translated from the German language—the language into which the meditation verses were brought by Rudolf Steiner from the spiritual world. In the mantric use of words, we have to do not only with their more obvious and current dictionary meaning but with their sound and rhythmic cadence and with the overtones of meaning that pervade them from the more lasting spirit of the language—from its forgotten past and yet unfathomed future.

1. These studies have been republished recently under the title *Christ and Sophia: Anthroposophic Meditations on the Old Testament, New Testament, and Apocalypse* (Gt. Barrington, MA: SteinerBooks, 2006).

Rudolf Steiner, as is well known, in an unprecedented way forges the German language into a vehicle for the expression of esoteric contents, and in so doing lets himself be bound by no conventions. The very absence of precise style and binding form, which has so often been criticized both in the language and in the peoples who speak it, becomes for one who is an initiate the possibility of shaping words and forms of speech freely to voice the Spirit. For here new spiritual life is entering humanity, and therefore quite new activities of mind and soul have to be invoked for its reception.

Rudolf Steiner brings something universally human into the language of spiritual science and makes it available for spiritual use—as for example Hebrew, Greek, and Sanskrit have been in other times and climes—to multitudes who in the ordinary way would have neither occasion nor aptitude to learn it. However, there are many of his students who have to rely on translations of his books, lectures, and meditative sayings. Therefore I will take this opportunity to mention some relevant points. For it is clear that in the mind of the writer, Valentin Tomberg, the original words will have called forth imaginations and thoughts that even the best available translation cannot evoke in quite the same way. Herein lies the difficulty of translating such a commentary.

The Foundation Stone consists of four verses. The first three concern the threefold human being (the focal centers of these three being head, heart, and limbs); also, the first three verses invoke the Divine Powers working into and through the human being. These three verses are followed by a fourth verse, which initially refers to the mystery of the Divine Birth at Christmas and then becomes a prayer addressing the birth of Christ within. Moreover, each of these first three verses is in two parts, the first of which exhorts the human soul to practice Spirit recollection in the first verse, to practice Spirit awareness in the second verse, and to practice Spirit beholding in the third verse.

In the fourth verse Christ sacrifices himself for the sake of humanity, bestowing meaning upon the Earth and upon the lives of human beings. Through this sacrifice, He brought meaning to human existence upon the Earth. The implication here is not only that Christ brings meaning to humanity and the entire evolution of the Earth, but also that without Him earthly life and history would remain meaningless. There is yet another aspect to this—that of Christ uniting with the Earth to bring the kingdom of heaven to Earth, without which there is no higher meaning or purpose to existence. Without Christ, Nature remains *maya* (the Sanskrit word for illusion). With Christ, however, nature is sanctified by His coming.

GEORGE ADAMS

THE
FOUNDATION STONE
MEDITATION

Human Soul!
Thou livest in the limbs
Which bear thee through the World of Space
Into the Spirit's Ocean Being.
Practice *Spirit Recollection*
In depths of soul,
Where in the Wielding Will
  of World Creating
Thine own I
Comes to being in God's I.
And thou wilt truly *live*
In Human World Being.

For the Father Spirit
  of the Heights holds sway
In Depths of Worlds
Begetting Being:
Seraphim, Cherubim, Thrones!
Let there ring out from the Heights
What in the Depths is echoed.

This speaks:
Ex Deo nascimur.

The Spirits of the Elements hear it:
In East, West, North, South—
May human beings hear it.

Human Soul!
Thou livest in the beat of heart and lung
Which leads thee through the Rhythm of Time
Into the realm of thine own soul's feeling.
Practice *Spirit Awareness*
In balance of the soul,
Where the Surging Deeds
  of the World's Becoming
Thine own I
Unite with the World I.
And thou wilt truly *feel*
In Human Soul Weaving.

For the Christ Will
  in the encircling Round holds sway
In Rhythms of Worlds
Bestowing Grace on the soul:
Kyriotetes, Dynamis, Exusiai!
Let there be fired from the East
What in the West is formed.

This speaks:
In Christo morimur.

The Spirits of the Elements hear it:
In East, West, North, South—
May human beings hear it.

Human Soul!
Thou livest in the resting head
Which from the Grounds of Eternity
Opens to thee the World Thoughts.
Practice *Spirit Beholding*
In stillness of thought,
Where the Eternal Aims of Gods
World Being's Light
On thine own I bestow
For thy free willing.
And thou wilt truly *think*
In Human Spirit Foundations.

For the World Thoughts
   of the Spirit hold sway
In Beings of Worlds
Beseeching Light:
Archai, Archangeloi, Angeloi!
Let there be prayed from the Depths
What in the Heights will be granted.

This speaks:
Per Spiritum Sanctum reviviscimus.

The Spirits of the Elements hear it:
In East, West, North, South—
May human beings hear it.

At the turning point of time
The Spirit Light of the World
Entered the Stream of Earthly Being.
Darkness of Night had held its sway.
Day-radiant Light streamed into human souls:
Light that gives warmth
To simple Shepherds' Hearts.
Light that enlightens
The wise Heads of Kings.

O Light Divine,
O Sun of Christ,
Warm Thou our hearts,
Enlighten Thou our heads,
That Good may become –
What from our hearts we found
And from our heads direct
With single purpose.

RUDOLF STEINER

When now, at this moment, we unite these three forces, the forces of the heights, the forces of the circumference, the forces of the depths, in a substance that gives form, then in the understanding of our soul we can bring face to face the universal dodecahedron with the human dodecahedron. Out of these three forces: out of the spirit of the heights, out of the force of Christ in the circumference, out of the working of the Father, the creative activity of the Father that streams out of the depths, let us at this moment give form in our souls to the dodecahedral Foundation Stone which we lower into the soil of our souls so that it may remain there a powerful sign in the strong foundations of our soul existence. . . .[2]

2. Rudolf Steiner, *The Christmas Conference, Part II: The Proceedings of the Conference 25 December 1923.*

PART 1

RESULTS OF WORKING
WITH THE FOUNDATION STONE MEDITATION

FOREWORD

THIS MEDITATION was given by Rudolf Steiner at the Christmas Foundation Meeting, 1923, as a spiritual Foundation Stone to the members of the worldwide Anthroposophical Society, newly founded at that time.

The author has for the past eleven years not only regarded it as the foundation stone of all anthroposophical study, but has endeavored to make it the foundation of all his written or spoken work. In whatever task he has had to perform, he has taken the Foundation Stone as his guide. It has proved an invaluable help; and the following work is intended as an expression of gratitude for that help—an expression of gratitude to Rudolf Steiner.

VALENTIN TOMBERG
TALLINN, ESTONIA
NOVEMBER, 1936

1

PAST, PRESENT, AND FUTURE

AS GATEWAYS TO THE SPIRITUAL WORLD

THE HUMAN CONSCIOUSNESS of the present-day knows itself to be immersed in the stream of time. It is not conscious of the time-stream as such, however, but only that that stream is flowing through it. The time-stream itself in its completeness does not appear to our consciousness: it springs from an unknown nothingness and vanishes into another nothingness. The darkness from which it springs is called the 'future'; the darkness into which it disappears is called the 'past'. The fact of being flowed through, experienced by human consciousness, is bound up with our notion of the 'present'.

This, fundamentally, is how time is experienced in the present phase of consciousness; however, if we are to take into account not only the bright light and the strong coloring, but also the feeble, shimmering light and the pale tints, then what has just been said must be to some extent modified. For in the darkness of the future a dim light of 'future *possibilities*' does indeed shimmer, and the searchlight of *remembrance* throws the fading colors of memory over part of the darkness of the past. Thus the transition from nothingness into visible appearance, and out of visible appearance into nothingness, is in reality not so abrupt: the future gleams dimly as 'possibility' and 'probability', and the past flows on a little farther in memory, before—gradually fading—it completely disappears. Yet even if the boundaries are not so clear-cut and the transitions are softened, nevertheless in the stream of time our human consciousness has a fragmentary character. And this is something felt by consciousness itself to be unsatisfying: we must *admit* our limitations,

3

but we cannot approve them. Indeed, it is inherent in the nature of human consciousness to strive to overcome these limitations. The very existence of religion and philosophy is enough to show that consciousness cannot reconcile itself to a permanent position between two darknesses. Even the *carpe diem*[1] of the Epicureans and the preaching of *Ecclesiastes* point to this; for if the human consciousness were normally satisfied with its position, there would be no occasion to exhort it to contentment, or preach a cheerful acceptance of what is given.

Now there is deep cause for the dissatisfaction of the human soul with its situation within the time-stream. The reason why the human soul thus faced with this fragmentary experience of time feels constrained to say that this indeed is so, but that it *ought not be so*, must be sought in the fact that the cleavage of time is a symptom of illness in human consciousness. For this cleavage of time is a consequence of the Fall. It was *Lucifer* who divided the unbroken circle of the time-stream into past and future, and this resulted in the *fleeting moment*, and in its consequences—error, but also freedom.

Since then, the human being's active life has been forever in the fleeting moment, only divining the future, only remembering the past. Yet since then there has also lived in the human soul a striving to transcend the boundary set by memory in the past and thereby overcome the darkness of forgetting, to transform the vague foreboding of the future into certainty of vision, and to reach beyond the fleeting glory of the moment to the true being of the ever-present. Wrestling with the dark forgetfulness of the past, awakening in the present through 'spirit-awareness', and beholding the future—herein consists the unremitting activity of human consciousness. And insofar as a soul is able to overstep these limitations, to that extent may we speak of the *greatness* of a human soul. What we admire in the character of a genius is the power to pierce through the semblance of the moment, to point out paths into the future, and to re-awaken the past. The *growth* of a soul consists in the widening of these boundaries of consciousness. And homage

---

1. *Carpe diem* means 'seize the day', implying that one should make the most of current opportunities because life is short. [ED]

given to any great soul is proof that the souls of all men and women yearn after growth. For this reason the Foundation Stone, which has for its content the general growth of the human soul, is addressed to the soul of every human being. The phrase opening each verse of the Meditation and characterizing its theme is *Human Soul!*

The Foundation Stone consists of thoughts concerning the ways and means of growth in the human soul, and the ways and means of help afforded to it by the spiritual world. Thus the first part of each of the three verses contains the instruction most essential to the human soul in order that it regain the past, find light in the future, and have its share in fundamental Being even in the fleeting glory of the present. The practice of *spirit-recollection, spirit-awareness,* and *spirit-beholding* form the content of the first half of each of the three verses. They contain that which the human soul must of necessity do *from within* in order to advance in the right direction.

The first of these three practices or exercises is concerned with an inward effort to alter the direction of the force of memory. For the direction in which memory commonly runs is horizontal. If we want to remember the past, we generally start from the present and think farther and farther back until we find the point we are seeking. This is the method of consciousness in the usual process of memory. And it is characteristic of this process that memory loses its strength when it has to go far into the past.

The call to practice *spirit-recollection* is not concerned however with lengthening the horizontal line of recollection but with a change of direction in the force of memory. The first step in meditation must indeed be the exclusion of all ordinary remembering. The activity of ordinary remembering must be brought to a standstill— this is the very first thing to be done. The horizontal line of memory must be contracted to a point; and all that is needed is that we recollect our own existence. When this stage of concentration is reached and the forces of consciousness are mustered, the next step is to give to the forces of memory a *vertical* direction. This means that we must no longer be remembering this, that, or the other, but must make our own higher nature, our own true Being, the object of our recollection. The light-stream of consciousness is now directed on the highest and deepest principle of our own humanity.

Then it may happen that the essential characteristics of a new nature gradually dawn on the consciousness of those practising this exercise, who cannot help recognizing this nature as their own, though it is utterly different from all that their ordinary experience has shown them of themselves.

For if hitherto the conception of our physical form and the idiosyncrasies of our soul-life have *set us apart* from the cosmic whole, *distinguishing* us from other beings within it, we now experience an active though tranquil nature, which instead of severing us from the cosmic whole *unites* us with it. It is a cosmic nature which, penetrating deeply and forcefully into our body, participates in the formation of that body, and by penetrating into the bodily limbs unites them with cosmic morality. The limb-system, which in the body merely consists of the members that carry the human soul through the world of space, becomes in this higher nature a cosmic will current, uniting the human soul with the surrounding Spirit-sea—the 'Spirit's Ocean Being'.

The physical legs on which we are supported and by means of which we stand clear of the solid earth-surface correspond to the will-currents that unite us with the earth and with its destiny. The arms, with which we hold and let loose, are, in the true nature of our human being, currents of a will for universal union, for the all-embracing harmony of the wide cosmic horizons. Even the head, which itself possesses some characteristics of a limb, becomes in this nature the upward-flowing current of devotion to the Divine Will.

The deep content of these will-currents—which flow through the height, depth, and breadth of the Universe, uniting the human being with the cosmos in every direction—is expressed with wonderful significance in the first three petitions of the Lord's Prayer. For the will-streams of this being are in fact not desires but *petitions*, addressed to the Divine Being on whom the world is founded. The upward stream can be expressed in the words 'Hallowed be thy Name'; the outward-flowing current of the will to universal union may be characterized by the words 'Thy Kingdom come'; and the downward current can find expression in the words 'Thy Will be done on Earth, as it is done in Heaven.'

This experience of spirit-recollection produces a change in the whole life-feeling of the human soul. It gives rise to a sense of being firmly planted within the current of the cosmic will-power's moral sway. We learn, for instance, to say the words 'I am' with new meaning. Instead of saying 'I am' in such a way that the utterance carries with it a *contrast* to an unexpressed 'Not I', it now becomes possible to say the 'I am' so that a world behind and above the 'I' may be divined. Then the 'I am' springs forth like a tongue of fire from the ocean of cosmic flame. For it is then no longer spoken *horizontally*, as a separate point upon an alien surface, but *vertically*—the coming into being of the 'I' within the 'I' of God.

The coming into being of our own 'I' within the Divine 'I' is the experience to which spirit-recollection, spiritual memory, can lead. Through this experience the human soul learns to know the nature of the past. By finding entrance to eternity in the past through spirit-recollection, the soul perceives the destiny of the past. The soul now recognizes that the past does not vanish into nothingness; it only loses its time-character and becomes *space*. Even the akashic record is supersensible space—it is all present at one and the same time. But physical space also comes into existence when the past becomes space. Expressions of the will of beings—deeds at one time or other in the fluctuation of creative happenings—become the content of the akashic record. But there are other streams of will whose aim is immobility and constancy of state. These become physical space, bodily form. Just as there are living thoughts that keep unbroken pace with creative metamorphoses, and on the other hand immobile, dogmatic thoughts rigidified into *formulas*, so also are there creative deeds, phases of an activity in constant metamorphosis, and also deeds whose impulse is to remain final and unaltered. An immobile and rigidified will produces physical matter and material bodies; physical bodies are 'dogmas of will', even as dogmas are mineralized thoughts. The stone is hard, not only because intermolecular attraction is strong in it, but because a constant and rigid will binds it together.

Moreover the members of the human space-body are rigidified will-currents of this kind. They are the past—of which the soul, a being of the present, makes use on its way to the future, which is the spirit.

For if all the past—even the supersensible past—becomes *body*, all the future is *spirit*, then it is only in the present that we actually have to do with the *soul*. The 'time-stream' we began by describing in the way the soul experiences it today is *in reality* not a horizontal current flowing from the future, through the present, to the past, but is the process, in which the soul participates, of spirit becoming body. The 'time-stream' *is*, in its reality, the descent of spirit into body. This process can be roughly shown by the following diagram.

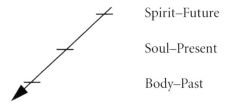

Spirit–Future

Soul–Present

Body–Past

We obtain in this way an idea more consistent with the reality of what we commonly call the 'flow of time', and we can also better understand why the future appears to us as dark: it appears dark because it is the spiritual world! Thus, for example, the seer who wrote the Apocalypse saw in the elemental world what he told us concerning the 'seven letters', whereas he found in the astral world what he wrote in connection with the 'seven seals', while the events he described as the sounding of 'seven trumpets' belonged to the 'devachanic' world, and the description of the 'seven vials of wrath' is derived from a still more exalted spiritual world. Now the 'seven letters' refer to the seven culture-epochs of Post-Atlantean civilization—that is, of the fifth great period—while the 'seven seals' refer to the sixth, and the 'seven trumpets' to the seventh great period. The 'vials of wrath' correspond to a still more distant future, namely, the end of the Earth-evolution and the transition to the Jupiter period.[2] This example given by St. John the Evangelist shows us *what* the future really is—that is, the descent of the spiritual world to earth.

2. See Rudolf Steiner, *The Apocalypse of Saint John: Lectures on the Book of Revelation* [GA 104], Anthroposophic Press, 1993, lectures 1 and 8.

This idea of time also shows us why the past appears dark to ordinary consciousness. It is because it becomes space. Space can be penetrated by the light of consciousness only when we recollect the spiritual process that gives rise to it. The human 'I', which 'comes to being in God's "I"', is also a part of space, but it is the one tract of space within the physical world, the world of things that *have* come into being, that is itself forever still in process of becoming—coming into being, deriving being, from the 'I' of God. The 'I' is both a *form* and also the unceasingly creative forming of this form; it is will, self-determining not once and for all but ever and again. The *existence* of the 'I' is no mere given fact, but spiritual activity, ever-enduring and creative.

Moreover it is creative activity, both of the 'I' itself and also of the Divine Foundation, God's 'I', within which the 'I' comes to being. It is important to understand that the 'I' does not merely exist or 'be', but is forever *coming into being*. The German word *erweset* ('comes to being') expresses a concept by means of which we can understand most deeply the nature of the human 'I'. Yet in the practice of *spirit-recollection* it is not enough to understand the nature of the human 'I': it must become vital *experience*. And this experience throws light upon the origin of space itself. Whatever is spatial originates in the same way as the human 'I'. But the spatial remains as it is once it has originated, whereas the 'I' continues to originate.[3] This is because the 'I' belongs not only to the past but also to the *present*. It is not only a past, but a past that is forever *becoming*—and this becoming is the spiritual reality of the present.

Now in order to grasp the spiritual reality of the present, the human soul must practise the exercise contained in the first half of the *second* verse of the Foundation Stone. It is the practice of *spirit-awareness* that enables the soul to become conscious of the living *reality* of the present. If the practice of spirit-recollection consists in giving the force of memory a new direction, practice of spirit-

---

3. In a lecture, which unfortunately the author has not at present beside him, Rudolf Steiner said that the human 'I' bears within itself the whole of the mineral world. If the human 'I' were to explode and disintegrate into space, from its fragments would arise the multiplicity of the mineral world. [See p 50, fn 2. ED]

awareness is also concerned with an alteration of ordinary experience—with a vital alteration of our experience in the *present*. In ordinary consciousness the present is experienced in such a way that the human soul is aware only of one bright point in the ever-flowing stream of time. The object of this second exercise is to become conscious not simply of the passing moment but of the presence of the spiritual, and this reaches far beyond the bright point experienced as the fleeting moment. Therefore the soul practicing spirit-awareness must try to extend the bright point to an ever-growing *sphere*. The human soul must learn to face the *cosmic present*, must learn to say, 'At this moment I stand within a World-constellation. I belong to it with my whole being. My breathing and my heartbeat have as large a share in the structure of this constellation as the sun and planets. The harmony of the stars, the sun, my heart, my breathing, and my feeling produce the constellation of the moment. The tide of the cosmic hour flows through my breast as well as through the heavenly spaces.' These and similar thoughts can give solemnity to the moment. We can then experience how our breast expands and our breathing is transformed. We breathe in time with the cosmos and our soul expands in concentric circles of solemn tranquility. But these concentric waves do not beat upon emptiness; they encounter waves of still deeper solemnity flowing from the heart of the universe. And in this encounter the human heart and the cosmic heart unite. Then the human soul may reflect: Every moment receives blessing from the heart of the world, without our being aware of it.

Thus we extend the feeling of our own soul-being, by the practice of spirit-awareness 'in balance of the soul', to realize our union with the 'I' of the world in the surging waves of cosmic evolution. Thereby we overcome the loneliness of life on earth. We no longer feel forsaken, for we know that in the widened horizon of the sun-filled meditative life we may even now share in the blessing that flows from the heart of the world. Thus the human soul learns true *feeling* from the feeling of the cosmos.

But from the cosmos the human soul also learns true *thinking*, and this arises from the experience to which the practice of *spirit-beholding* leads. For the practice of spirit-beholding, described in

the first half of the *third* verse of the Foundation Stone, contains all
the instruction the soul needs for learning to think truly, which is
what the human soul must do in order to see into the *future*. For
thinking is indeed the faculty that even in our everyday experience
of time throws some degree of light onto the darkness of the future.
And so it is also the faculty by means of which we may expect to
attain certainty of vision, penetrating into the future. In order to
attain this, as radical a change must be made in the force of thought
as in the force of memory by the practice of spirit-recollection, and
in that of feeling by the practice of spirit-awareness. We can understand this transformation of thinking that takes place in the practice
of spirit-beholding if we realize that in the normal state of consciousness thinking is also like memory. Only, it is a recollection
that *divines* the possibilities of the future, whereas memory consists
in honoring the facts of the past.

When directed to the future, ordinary thinking likewise moves in
a horizontal line, since it takes its start from the past, and from the
past draws conclusions about the future. But it still remains for the
most part uncertain; for even in endeavoring to draw a line from the
past into the future—that is, to guess at the future on the basis of the
highest *probability*—it still has the hypothetical character of conjec-
ture. Now, hypothesis as such is neither a pure question addressed
to the spiritual world nor yet clear knowledge. It is therefore apt
rather to place itself between the truth and human consciousness—
concealing more than revealing the truth. For real knowledge of the
truth, *problems* are necessary—that is to say, questions wherein the
soul is sincerely ready for *every* answer. For real discovery of knowledge, the questions must not contain in themselves anything that
dictates the answer. As regards the content of the answer, the question must preserve a *silence* ready to meet whatever comes. Thought
must be *free of hypotheses* if it is to lead to sure knowledge. It must
therefore *refrain* from answering itself. It must be content with the
role of stating the problem in a mature and balanced manner, and
then awaiting the answer in silence.

It is precisely this silent waiting of the *active* thinking-faculty for
which the practice of spirit-vision or 'spirit-beholding' strives. Just
such a lull must be induced in the ordinary hypothesizing thought-

activity as takes place in the normal horizontal course of remembering during the practice of 'spirit-recollection'. Here too the aim is to alter the direction of the thinking faculty. In the practice of spirit-beholding the point is to change the thought-direction from the horizontal of hypothesis to the vertical of vision—a change that consists in directing the thinking faculty *upward*. It is not directed upward, however, in the sense that one's own opinions are projected into the heavens, but in the sense of a calm, clear-seeing *gaze*. Scattered and restless thought-activity must be collected and converged into a silent *faculty of penetrating vision*. When this happens—that is, when the calm gaze of the thinking faculty is directed upwards— a knowledge free of hypothesis is achieved. We have contributed nothing towards it from our own subjective self. We no longer cogitate; we behold. As a flower that I see with my eyes is no creation of fancy, so what is seen in this 'stillness of thought' is no hypothesis; it is no more dependent on the arbitrary human will than is the flower perceived by the eye. It is the cosmic thoughts, seen by the human soul. When we transform our own thinking faculty into a calm, seeing eye, we become aware of the thought-power of the universe. And on the cosmic thoughts, seen in this way, we can then model and orient our own. Thus the human soul learns to think truly by learning from the thinking of the gods.

For the future *is* the thinking of the gods. The flow of the future into the present and into the past is nothing else than the realizing of divine thoughts—of the 'eternal aims of gods'. Whether in a pure unsullied form, or in a caricatured or even antagonistic form, it is still the descent of divine thoughts into earthly reality. Whether the realization of the divine aims is pure or caricatured or changed into its antithesis, depends on the free will of the human being, standing between good and evil. Yet the real *content* of it always originates in the thinking of the gods, quite irrespective of the *use* that free beings may make of it. The gods *bestow* the light of their cosmic thoughts upon free beings for their free will and choice. They give it in confidence that the sublime *content* of these thoughts will speak for itself, and that the beings upon whom they are bestowed will be worthy of them.

2

THE CROSS OF SPACE

REVELATION-CURRENTS
OF THE SPIRITUAL WORLD

THE FIRST HALF of the first three verses of the Foundation Stone contain what the human soul must do *from within* in order to pass through the gates of past, present, and future—in thinking, feeling, and willing—into direct and conscious union with the spiritual world. The second half contains what the *spiritual world* does to help the human soul, for the growth of the human soul results from the cooperation of the soul itself with the spiritual world. The effort of the practising soul is the *one* side of the process; the help given by the spiritual world in response to the soul's activity is the *other*.

This other side of the intercourse of the human soul with the spiritual world also occurs in three directions. For the same three gates by which the human soul reaches the spiritual world are used by the spiritual world to reach the human soul. The *revelation* of the spiritual world can only take place along the same paths, where from the human side *knowledge* is being sought and striven for. Thus there are in the universe three currents that reveal the spiritual world and enrich the willing, feeling, and thinking of the human soul.

The first of these streams of revelation is that which flows from the fount of *eternity in the past*. For there are *three* such well-springs of eternity, and we make contact with them when we reach out to the spirit through the gateways of the past, the present, and the future. Through these three gates the human soul gains knowledge of eternity. Through the gateway of the past we acquire knowledge of God the Father, through the gateway of the present we realize the presence of God the Son, and through the gateway of the future we are illumined by the rays of God the Holy Spirit.

The Father-God, actively, creatively at work, is only to be found revealed in the past. In the present and the future the Father-Being is not revealed. The Father-God has been at rest since He conceived those cosmic thoughts that are the beings of the universe. The Father-Being remains at rest outside and above all worlds that have arisen, are arising, or shall yet arise; He cannot therefore be found within those worlds. He stands above existence, engendering existence—'begetting being'—and is thus Himself beyond being. He can, therefore, never be an *object* of knowledge. For the life of *knowledge*, the Father-Being is an eternal secret.

Yet though He is to *knowledge* an eternal secret, nevertheless beings who stand at the threshold of cosmic existence can make the Father-God the content of their *revelation*. They can bring *tidings* of the Father and of the mysteries of His providence. Such tidings sound forth in the depths of the human will-nature, which we tried to characterize in speaking of the practice of spirit-recollection. The beings of the First Hierarchy pour into the essence of human will the sustaining *forces* of the tidings of God the Father. Thrones, Cherubim, and Seraphim respond, with the activity of divine moral forces, to the three 'petitions', which sound forth as living streams of will from the depths of our will-nature. The will-stream of the 'head' is illumined by the Cherubim, the will-stream of the 'arms' is warmed through and through by the Seraphim, the will-stream of the 'legs' receives force and direction from the Thrones.

These functions of the Spirits of Will (Thrones), the Spirits of Harmony (Cherubim), and the Spirits of Love (Seraphim) produce impulses in the will-nature that has come under their influence. The impulses that resound into our conscious life out of the depths of our will-nature are a reflection, an *echo*, of these divine activities. This echo makes itself heard as a chord of *three* notes. The first note tells of the Divine Being, exalted far above the cosmos; the second note proclaims the brotherly and sisterly unity of the beings who share this common origin; the third speaks of all that has come into being from that Divine Father-realm beyond the world.

The echo of the working of the Spirits of Harmony reveals the tidings of the divine; the activity of the Spirits of Will is heard in the echo of the recollection of our coming-into-being out of the divine; the working of the Spirits of Love sounds forth in the brotherly and sisterly integration in community of all those who have thus come into being from the divine. The harmony of the three-toned echo of the combined activities of the First Hierarchy's revealing power is expressed in human speech in the words of the Foundation Stone:

From the Divine, humanity comes to being.[1]

And the inner meaning of this line can be immeasurably deepened by thinking of it as consisting of three parts, and bringing each of these parts into relation with one of the three Hierarchies of the cosmic Spirits of Strength:

From the Divine—Revelation of the Spirits of Harmony
humanity—Outpouring of the Spirits of Love
comes to being—Deed of the Spirits of Will.

If the Father-Spirit of the Heights is out of reach of direct knowledge, it is otherwise with the relationship of the human soul to the Son. The Son is *met* by the human soul when, as a result of the practice of spirit-awareness, the gateway of the present has been passed. For if the human soul expands its present experience from a point outward to the cosmic circumference—the 'encircling round'—it meets the Christ-will by which the soul is blessed. The Divine Son works *in* the world, and therefore it is possible to meet Him in the world, and indeed to meet Him as an individual Being. The *Christ-Being* is no 'principle', but the heart of the universe—or, what is the same thing, the spiritual sun of the universe. And the word is not used in the sense of an organism or fixed star, but in the sense of a Being holding the central position in the moral and spiritual space of the universe.

---

1. These words express in English Rudolf Steiner's rendering of the expression *Ex Deo nascimur.* [ED]

As the existence of the visible sun can be realized in two ways—either by seeing its light and feeling its warmth, or by looking directly at it in the sky—so also the reality of Christ can be experienced in two ways, either by feeling the *effect* of the soul-blessing rhythm of His Will prevailing in the encircling round, or by direct meeting with His essential *Being*. The first way is open to all; the second is a *visitation of grace*, not to be attained by effort but only to be hoped for. The experiencing of the spiritual Sun's life-giving light in the rhythms of the universe is a stage on the path of spiritual training, but the experience of meeting with the Christ Himself—as, for instance, St. Paul did on the road to Damascus—is an *act* of grace bestowed by Christ Himself.

The shedding of light by the spiritual Sun of the universe is not an inert, automatic radiation, but a conscious, rhythmical breathing of the Christ-force into the working of the world by means of hierarchic being. The 'rays' of the Christ-light in the world do not run in *straight* lines like the Luciferic light-rays of the visible sun; they flow through the universe in rhythmical waves of circular and spiral-looping motion. The spiritual light of the Christ-Sun flows through the world in accordance with definite forms of movement. For in these rays the Spirits of Form (Exusiai or Elohim), the Spirits of Movement (Dynamis), and the Spirits of Wisdom (Kyriotetes) have a share. The Spirits of Wisdom member the light into rays in the wisest way; the Spirits of Movement carry it to the beings in the world; the Spirits of Form mould the rhythmic shape of its movement.

The three hierarchies of the cosmic Spirits of Light bring the fire, the movement, and the form of the life-giving Light of Christ into the life of earth. Moreover they bring it—as a *cosmic*[2] current—in the *horizontal* direction that is from sunrise to sunset. This horizontal cosmic current expresses simultaneously the graduated working of the three Hierarchies of the Spirits of Light. For the activity of the Spirits of Wisdom preponderates in the East—the current having

---

2. We are here speaking of the working of the *cosmic* stream; the corresponding current of the spiritual *Earth-organism* has a different direction.

there the quality of pure spiritual Fire drawing near the earth. Then, as the current flows further towards the West, the Spirits of Move-ment begin to participate in it, making it spiritual light that moves our moral feeling; while in the West—through the preponderance of the Spirits of Form—it becomes definite spiritual missions, tasks, and aims to be achieved on earth. In the West the current reaches its destination; through the spiritual forces of the West it can become a reality helping to mould the destiny of the earth; it here receives a *form* corresponding to the earth's destiny.

And then its ever moving wisdom-content is formed or moulded into the great words of revelation. What moved as a kindling fire from East to West now becomes *speech*; and in this speech rings forth the revelation of the cosmic and earthly activity of Christ. It contains three 'words': the word of *Christ* as the ideal *archetype* of all individual beings; the word of His grace-bestowing *Life*; and the word proclaiming that death also is included in this gift of grace.

The word of the Spirits of Form reveals the moral *power* of Christ as the archetype and prototype of all beings; the word of the Spirits of Movement reveals the inner *might* of Christ as the life-spring of the universe; and the Spirits of Wisdom reveal the bounds of his *dominion* as extending even beyond the realm of death. So closely allied is the activity of the Spirits of Light with the revelation of Christ that the Christians of the first centuries called the three Hier-archies by the names of those qualities of the Christ-Being that each reveals: they named them *Powers* (Exusiai), *Mights* (Dynamis), and *Dominions* (Kyriotetes).

The formed revelation of the combined hierarchies of the Spirits of Light gives rise to the saying of the Foundation Stone:

In Christ death becomes life.[3]

In this saying the three revelations concerning Christ flow together, and we deepen our relation to it when we think of it artic-ulated in this way:

---

3. These words express in English Rudolf Steiner's rendering of the expression *In Christo morimur.* [ED]

In Christ—the ultimate Ideal, declared by the Spirits of Form
death—the Dominion, proclaimed by the Spirits of Wisdom
becomes life—the Well-spring of Life, revealed by the Spirits
of Movement.

The gateway leading to the experience of the Holy Spirit as the
eternal in the future is passed through by means of the practice of
spirit-beholding, spirit-penetrating vision. The future is then
revealed in the form of cosmic thoughts. They express the eternal
aims of gods within the scope of human consciousness intently gaz-
ing in stillness of thought. It is the *will* of the spirit-world, making
itself known through cosmic thoughts. This will becomes thought
within the human spirit-being—the spirit-self (*manas*)—which
offers up human thinking activity as an arena for the will of the
spirit-world. The 'higher-eye' of the spirit-self perceives the divine
aims and purposes, making them its own and moulding them into
thoughts. The 'lower eye' of 'stillness of thought' beholds these
thoughts. However, this seeking makes a twofold claim on the consciousness of the beholder, who on the one hand must be capable of
perceiving the cosmic thoughts, and on the other must be in a position to *understand* them, that is, to make them his or her own. If it
were solely a question of perception, the cosmic thoughts would
have significance for human consciousness only so long as it is in
the state of spiritual vision. When not in this state, human consciousness could no longer retain the cosmic thought as its own
property of knowledge, for it would not be associated with this
former knowledge in thought or in experience. It would remain
simply a dream-like memory.

In order that what is spiritually seen may at the same time be
understood—that is, fruitfully incorporated into the whole
thought-content of consciousness—there must be a higher degree
of *wakefulness* in the human soul than would be necessary for perception alone. Now the measure of wakefulness is nothing other
than the measure of the *light* of consciousness illumining the soul.
This light—the light of the soul's wakefulness—flows unceasingly
from the fount of the *Holy Spirit*, working by means of the spiritual
hierarchies. The stream of the Holy Spirit, awakening the beings of

the world, is continually flowing through the human soul, but consciousness becomes more *wakeful* when the soul *receives* this stream by its own activity. The activity consists primarily in the soul producing *questions* from within itself. By this means the stream enters the consciousness of the soul, making it more intense. Then the soul is more awake than before.

This increased wakefulness is precisely the effect produced upon the soul by 'spirit-beholding' of the cosmic thoughts. It is not only a question of the soul *seeing* these thoughts, but of its bringing so much light to bear on them that they can enter into the soul's consciousness without being overcome by darkness. Hence there are two sides to spirit-beholding: not only are cosmic thoughts perceived, but the *awakening* of the soul takes place at the same time. This is the gift of the Holy Spirit who, to the revelation of the eternal aims of gods, adds also the power to grasp them. Without this help from the flow of the Spirit, the cosmic thoughts would be entities longing for union with the soul yet unable to attain this union. They would be like bees seeking flowers but finding none.

Therefore the cosmic thoughts of the Spirit reign in the beings of the world, *beseeching* light. Their prayer is held aloft like a cup by the Spirits of Soul (the Third Hierarchy), and the pleading cup of cosmic thought is filled with the Holy Spirit and then poured out into the world below. By this means human souls are awakened.

The holding of the 'beseeching cup' gathering the light of soul-consciousness and its outpouring into the human soul, is the work of the Third Hierarchy, the hierarchy of the Holy Spirit. The Holy Spirit is not outside the world and beyond the power of perception, as is the Father, nor can the Holy Spirit be *met with* in the world, like the Son. It *fills* beings from within; the Holy Spirit is not an object of perception, but the inner possibility thereof. The reality of the Holy Spirit's existence is revealed by the *awakening* of the soul to new tasks, new spheres of life—even new worlds. And this awakening takes place through the activity of the Spirits of Soul, who receive the radiant light of the Holy Spirit and pour it into civilization, into groups of human beings, and into individuals. By this means men and women awaken to the tasks of their age, to social tasks, to their tasks as individuals. Through the activity of the

Angels the individual human being is awakened to his or her destiny; the Archangels awaken souls to one another; and the Archai, the Time-Spirits, are active in awakening human souls to the needs of the age in which they live. The Archai awaken the soul to world-concerns; the Angels help the soul to be awake to its own spiritual needs; and the Archangels awaken the soul to other souls. Thus the collaboration of the whole hierarchy of Spirits of Soul is expressed in the saying of the Foundation Stone:

In the world-thoughts of the Spirit, the soul awakens.[4]

Once more, our comprehension of these words can be deepened, when, in the word 'awakens', we find three stages:

The soul awakens—for itself—through the light of the Angels.
The soul awakens—for humanity—through the warmth of the Archangels.
The soul awakens—for the world—through the fire of the Archai.

4. These words express in English Rudolf Steiner's rendering of the expression *Per Spiritum Sanctum reviviscimus.* [ED]

3

SUMMARY

IN STUDYING THE FIRST THREE VERSES, expressing the assistance given by the spiritual world, we must bear in mind that the help of the spiritual world is *one and undivided*, though in *describing* these things it is impossible to do otherwise than separate them and study them singly. Yet in order to get an idea of the unity—of the streams of assistance both from the spiritual world and from the Foundation Stone meditation itself—it is important to study the first three verses not only from the standpoint of *time*—that is, as gateways to the past, the present, and the future—but also from the standpoint of *space*. For a study from the standpoint of space—that is, of juxta-position—always produces a more *synoptic* view than a study from the standpoint of time.

Not only the above consideration, but also the Foundation Stone meditation itself, leads to the spatial point of view. For each of the first three verses of the meditation contains a reference to the spatial aspect. Thus the Father-verse speaks of the call that rings forth from the *heights* and is echoed in the *depths*. This gives us the spatial direction *from above downward*. The Son-verse refers to the spatial direction *from East to West*, in the encircling round wherein the Christ-will holds sway. The Spirit-verse tells of the prayer from the *depths* that is heard in the *heights*: here we have the spatial direction *from below upward*.

Combining these space-directions—which are in fact currents of help and bounty from the spiritual world—we obtain the *cosmic cross* of space, the interplay of streams creating, healing, and enlightening the world. Against this background of the world there dawns upon the inner eye the symbol of the cosmic *Rose-Cross*, with the circle, where in the seven cosmic rhythms the meeting with the

Christ-will takes place, seen as a ring around the center of the cross. Thus the Foundation Stone meditation is not only an elaboration of the three Rose-Cross mantra;[1] it is actually based on the symbol of the Rose-Cross.

The spiritual currents from above downward, from East to West, and from below upward, are at the same time the content of the ancient Mystery-concepts of "East, West, North, and South." The *cosmic* North is the Father-being and the activity of the Father-hierarchies; the cosmic South is the Spirit and the hierarchies of the Spirit; the cosmic horizontal from East to West is the Son as *God-Man*, and His hierarchies.[2] These cosmic spiritual streams become *moral* facts of nature within the elemental world. The beings of the four elements—spirits of Earth, Water, Air, and Fire—hear the message of the heavenly directions, and the Foundation Stone meditation is given so that human souls may also hear them.

1. The three Rose-Cross mantra are: *Ex Deo nascimur, In Christo morimur, Per Spiritum Sanctum reviviscimus.* The first three verses of the Foundation Stone meditation are an elaboration on these three mantra. [ED]

2. It must here be repeated that we are speaking now of the directions of *cosmic* currents. The etheric *Earth-organism* has corresponding currents of its own, distinct from the cosmic currents.

PART 2

THE DEEPENING OF INNER LIFE BY MEANS
OF THE FOUNDATION STONE MEDITATION

FOREWORD

THE FOLLOWING PAGES comprising Part II are a continuation of the brief study on the Foundation Stone meditation published at Christmas 1936 (Part I). At that time my chief effort was to help stimulate an understanding of the more cosmic spiritual aspect of the meditation. In this second part I am more concerned with the aspect of *the inner life, the human soul.* In the third part I shall indicate how the Foundation Stone meditation relates to the Kingdoms of Nature.

VALENTIN TOMBERG
TALLINN, ESTONIA
CHRISTMAS, 1937

1

FREEDOM IN THE SPIRIT:

THE FOUNDATION OF INDIVIDUALITY

STUDYING OUR OWN NATURE from the physical side, we are bound to admit that in nothing are we more dependent on the outer world than in the necessity of breathing. Whether we wake or sleep, whether we are healthy or sick, young or old, we are always breathing, and constantly in need of the air the world offers us. In the same sense, the other pole of human nature—that is, the inner life of our being—is also dependent on the outer world. The human soul needs air, just as the body needs the air of the atmosphere. The 'air' the soul needs in order to be active and healthy is the spirit, whose in-flowing is as necessary to the soul as is the flow of air through the lungs to the body.

But there is an important distinction between the body's breathing of the air and the soul's breathing of the spirit. While the body's breathing functions of itself, so that it continues to breathe even in sleep, the soul's breathing no longer does so. There was a time in the far distant past when it also functioned of its own accord, but today it must be *learned*. Today, conscious initiative and effort are needed before the spirit can flow into the soul as the air flows into the body in breathing. And this initiative, this effort of the soul to throw itself open to the spirit, is precisely what spiritual science calls *meditation*. It is in meditation that we learn and practice this *other* kind of breathing, namely, the breathing of the soul within the spirit.

For the breathing of the soul in the spirit is the result of *conscious* relationship with the spirit during meditation—a relationship as direct as the unconscious relationship between the body and air. And the feeling that accompanies the inflow of the spirit into the soul during—or immediately after—meditation is the 'radiant breath of freedom'. A feeling of *emancipation* is the sign that the spirit has made contact with the soul and is flowing through it. This feeling is no illusion, but a real effect of a real cause. For it is the special function of meditation to cause the soul to devote itself no longer only to the philosophical *problem* of freedom but to the real *life-element* of freedom; precisely by *experiencing* it thus, we learn to solve the problem of freedom. Experience of freedom comes to the human soul through direct and conscious contact with the spiritual world.

To be in direct contact with the spiritual world is to experience freedom—the air and life-breath of the soul. There are a number of *indirect* relationships with the spiritual world: moral and philosophic dogmas, rules and precepts, human authorities, etc. These may all be good, but they do not give freedom to the soul. For they stand between the soul and the spiritual world, and the soul devotes itself to *them* instead of to the spiritual world, putting them in the place of the spiritual world and hence also of spiritual freedom. For this reason Rudolf Steiner prefaced his whole life-work by his writings on Goethe and by his *Philosophy of Freedom*.[1] For both Goethe's method and the *Philosophy of Freedom* are means of arriving at a *direct* relation to the spiritual world by removing all barriers built up between it and the human soul. The Goethean method leads to direct perception, to an unbiased seeing of the world around us; it is concerned not with what is said about the world but with the world itself. The 'open secret' of light, for example, is for Goethe not a thought-out formula, but the *word of revelation* resulting from our seeing the phenomena of light and their mutual relations. Similarly, the *Philosophy of Freedom* clears away all that obstructs the approach of the soul to freedom by basing knowledge on a direct vision from two sides: the percept and the intuition belonging to the percept. It bases the moral life also on a direct rela-

---

1. *Die Philosophie der Freiheit* [GA 4]. The later editions of the English translations were entitled—at Rudolf Steiner's request—*Philosophy of Spiritual Activity*. A still more recent English translation is entitled *Intuitive Thinking as a Spiritual Path*. [ED]

tion to the spiritual world, deriving ethical deeds not from adherence to rules but from the moral intuition reached through the medium of moral imagination. Rudolf Steiner's *Philosophy of Freedom* is the most effective method conceivable, not only to give the soul a real *idea* of freedom but also to clear away all hindrances that may prevent the soul from *experiencing* the reality of freedom. Indeed, the inner clarity and certainty that comes to the soul from simply thinking through the content of the *Philosophy of Freedom* is for many *in itself* such an experience of freedom that they can never forget it, and must always strive to go forward in the same direction. This striving fills the soul with mathematical certainty, and also a religious necessity felt by the heart to practise *meditation*.

For meditation is the realization in practice of what the *Philosophy of Freedom* describes as the adjustment of one's entire being to the true concept of freedom. In meditation we reach the condition characterized in the *Philosophy of Freedom* as that of a free being. Such a condition does not consist in the capacity to wish for this or that, but in the degree of *consciousness* with which a deed is carried out. In meditation this becomes experience, because meditation itself is a deed that can only be derived from, and carried out, in complete consciousness.

According to the approach of the *Philosophy of Freedom* and the experience of meditation, human beings can be free *only* insofar as they are *conscious*. Human beings reach ever higher stages of wakeful consciousness the more directly they live in the world from which the light of all consciousness issues, that is, the spiritual world.

This concept of freedom underlies Rudolf Steiner's spiritual science; and it is the same conception of freedom that underlies the gospels. For when Christ Jesus spoke the words from the cross: 'Father, forgive them, *for they know not what they do*,' He implied that they who did it were not yet free, because they did not know what they were doing and therefore could not be held responsible. Human beings are fully responsible when they *know* what they are doing, for only then are they free.

There is only one sin that cannot be forgiven: the sin against the Holy Spirit, that is, the *conscious* turning away from the fountainhead of consciousness.

The conception of freedom taught by spiritual science is, after all, the *real* conception of freedom taught by Christianity. Yet it is not nearly as widespread as Christianity outwardly is. *Other* conceptions of freedom—of non-Christian origin—have spread into the Christian world and have been so intensely fostered that the true Christian conception of it has been forgotten. These other ideas of freedom may in a general way be summarized from two points of view: the *Eastern* idea of freedom, and the *American*.

In the East—especially in India and Central Asia—freedom is regarded as signifying an emancipation *from* the bonds that bind the soul to the earth. We are free when we have *loosed* ourselves from all that is earthly. The Eastern idea of freedom is a condition of consciousness that has freed itself from the karmic stream of repeated earth-lives and is able to rest tranquilly outside them. To the Easterner, freedom is identical with emancipation from any connection with the sphere of earthly life. The world of deeds is not included in the sphere of freedom; it stands outside it. Deeds spring from necessities; so turns the wheel of destiny. The point is not that we should turn the wheel, but that we should *detach* ourselves from its turning. This can only be done when the light of consciousness is freed from the will-element (*kama* and *tanha*) that urges us to deeds. It is not a question of illumining the dark will-element, but of *severing* the higher human being from the lower. Concretely pictured, this emancipation of the higher human being from the lower would result in the head, with the chest and arms, freeing itself from the rest of the torso and soaring into the heights, while the lower parts of the human body remain behind.

The opposite is represented by the ideal of freedom pursued above all in America. The freedom striven after in America is freedom of the *will*. We are free when we can do what we will—this is the axiom of the American idea of freedom. To realize this ideal, the will must be strong enough to overcome the hindrances that bind it—and to overcome them by the help of intelligence, of the light of consciousness. Nature, for instance, must be mastered by the human will. The technical discoveries made by intelligence at the behest of will are so many steps towards realizing the ideal of freedom in the sense of *overcoming hindrances* that impede the human will. Pictured concretely, the realization of the American ideal of freedom would mean abnegating the functions of the head to the torso—the rest of the body engulfing the head, as it were.

Now the ideal presented at the beginning of this study shows neither a detachment of consciousness from will, nor a conquest of the world of will. In the Christian ideal of freedom, the will is illuminated by consciousness. For will in itself is not free; and consciousness in itself lacks deeds—it is the 'faith that is without works is dead.' Strength of will must be added to clear consciousness, thus making the dark, and hence unfree, will bright—that is, free—by the light of consciousness. The gospel precept 'Ye shall know the truth, and the truth shall make you free' underlies this purely *human* idea of freedom. The only *human* conception of freedom is realized in *deeds* inspired by the *spiritual world* and carried out on *earth*. For human beings are on earth to *act*; yet at the same time are *spiritual* beings, and as such have to act on earth.

We find this conception of freedom in the gospels; we find it at the root of Goethe's scientific method; we find it clearly thought out in Rudolf Steiner's *Philosophy of Freedom*. Moreover we find the fact of freedom presented with the same thoughtful clarity in the third verse of the Foundation Stone, where in the direct speech of spiritual experience the cosmic element of this experience comes to majestic expression.

> *Human Soul!*
> Thou livest in the resting head
> Which from the Grounds of Eternity
> Opens to thee the World Thoughts.
> Practice *Spirit Beholding*
> In stillness of thought,
> Where the Eternal Aims of Gods
> World Being's Light
> On thine own 'I' bestow
> For thy free willing.
> And thou wilt truly *think*
> In Human Spirit Foundations.

This part of the verse expresses, so to speak, the *method and technique* of the soul's experience of freedom, seen with its cosmic background. And indeed, freedom is brought about as the result both of what the human soul itself does, and of what the spiritual world brings to it. For the condition necessary to the experience of freedom is the spirit-beholding vision of the soul in the resting head's repose of thought. This condition is *meditation*, for meditation is the condition in which the soul passes over from thinking to the thought, and from the thought to absolute repose of thought. This 'stillness of thought' is however not mere absence of thought—it is the surrender of our own thought to cosmic thought. Cosmic thought now brings the eternal aims of gods to us, that we may make them our own, and pours into them the light of cosmic being, vouchsafed to the human 'I' for free and active will. By letting the light of the eternal aims of the gods shine into it, our will becomes free.

The human will *is* not free, but it can *become* free when illumined by the light of consciousness. And this illumining is the result of *true thinking*—thinking in which the vagaries of 'elaborated' thoughts are replaced by the certain *vision* of cosmic thoughts. Such thoughts are not abstractions but realities. For this reason they are not so ineffective in relation to the inner life of the human being as are abstract thoughts; they are efficacious even into the depths of the life of the will. The influence of cosmic thought on this whole nature of the human soul is shown in its gradual awaking—stage by stage, layer by layer, as it were.

This fact is expressed in the *second* part of the third verse, culminating in the sentence:

In the World-Thoughts of the Spirit the soul awakens.[2]

The sleeping soul is unfree; its awakening is freedom. The more awake a soul can become, the more free it is, and at the same time so

---

2. This is an English translation of Rudolf Steiner's rendering into German of the Latin Rosicrucian saying *Per spiritum Sanctum reviviscimus*, which is the culmination of the third verse of the Foundation Stone Meditation. [ED]

much the more responsible. The stages of awakening to the responsibility of freedom are the essential stages of initiation. Initiation is
the karmic test of our ripeness for the responsibility of the freedom
of an awakened consciousness. Initiation is at once the realization
of freedom and the *practical* solution of the philosophical problem
of freedom. Its stages are the stages of emancipation, and its trials
are tests of ripeness for the growing responsibility that growing
freedom brings.

2

UNITY IN THE SON

THE FOUNDATION
OF TRUE COMMUNITY

IF THE PRINCIPLE of individual initiation is *one* side of the Foundation Stone that Rudolf Steiner laid in the hearts of members at the Christmas Foundation Meeting, 1923, the other aspect of this Stone is the principle of *community*. Moreover, it is the principle of a community founded on the Spirit, which implies that the community must be founded neither on obligatory tenets (dogmas) nor on the mere pursuit of practical aims (interests), but on a life of knowledge such as will link human beings together in a free covenant.

Now the community-forming life of knowledge is something new and unknown; indeed, it is so foreign to European spiritual life that we can hardly approach it at all, save with such notions as might be applied either to a sect or a research institute. That there can be a community-forming life of knowledge that neither starts a sect nor founds a research institute is almost entirely beyond the sphere of our modern experience. We could even say that we cannot expect the forming of such a community to be an object of experience to modern men and women, since it is not a gift bestowed but a *task* still to be fulfilled. It is a task, moreover, the execution of which depends on the degree to which the Christ-impulse makes itself felt. For though the Christ-Impulse can indeed be *recognized* in and by the individual, it becomes a living reality only in relations between individuals. The gospel formula 'Where two or three are gathered together in my name, there am I in the midst of them' expresses the fundamental fact that the Christ-Impulse is effectively present upon earth in the *community*. The Christ-Impulse expresses

itself in life by uniting human beings together. And a life of knowledge permeated by the Christ expresses itself in like manner. It too
has a community-forming influence.

The life of knowledge permeated by the Christ-Impulse is, however, one in which *death* becomes *life*. Hence it is necessary that the
head's dead thought should be brought down into the heart, where
it becomes life. When it is brought down to the heart, it is changed
from a force that separates human beings into one that connects
them. Every true thought that has reached the heart becomes a
force of social healing; every thought—even the most true—that
remains in the head, hardens to dogma there and has an anti-social
influence. In *Knowledge of the Higher Worlds* Rudolf Steiner
expresses this in another way: 'Every idea that becomes an ideal for
you creates life forces in you, every idea that does not become an
ideal, slays the life-forces in you.' It is these very 'life-forces' that are
community-forming. For the Christ-Impulse works especially
through the life-body (the ether body) and, combining with *its* spiritual forces, brings about the good and true union of human beings,
whereas in the present age our astral body is thoroughly anti-social.
Everything 'personal' in us is anchored in our astral body, which is
thus not adapted to link human beings together in an *objectively*
spiritual way. The uniting power belongs rather to the life-body—
that is, to the ego experiencing consciously in the life-body. For
when the 'I' is living thus in the life-body, it acquires a sun-like
character, whereas in the astral body it dwells in a world of loneliness, and in a social sense can have only a feeble influence. The
forces of the astral body are *death-forces* for all that is social; yet
when brought down to the life-body these forces are thereby
changed into social life-forces. This change is effected by the Christ-
Impulse. And so the central lines of the second verse of the Foundation Stone also refer to the conversion of what is socially dead in the
astral body into what is socially alive in the ether-body.

For the saying 'In Christ death becomes life'[1] signifies in the first

---

1. This is an English translation of Rudolf Steiner's rendering into German of
the Latin Rosicrucian saying *In Christo morimur*, which is the culmination of the
second verse of the Foundation Stone Meditation. [ED]

instance, for the present sphere of human endeavor, the reanima-
tion of the dying life of knowledge.

The re-animation of the dying life of knowledge is the *other* side
of the Foundation Stone, adding to the principle of individual freedom that of *community*. For when the life of knowledge has
descended to the heart, by the very fact of becoming heart it
becomes a community-forming force. This is easily understood if
we compare the heart's supersensible mode of operation with that
of the head. In the functioning of the head the center is in the head
itself, raying forth influences that shine upon or penetrate into the
objects perceived. The heart functions in a different way. There the
center itself may even be outside in the surrounding sphere—'in the
encircling round'—whence it will pour back its knowledge to
human beings. This mode of operation of the microcosmic sun, the
heart, is a microcosmic counterpart of the macrocosmic Sun, the
Christ. It is expressed in the words of the meditation:

> For the Christ Will
> In the encircling Round holds sway
> In Rhythms of Worlds
> Bestowing Grace on the soul

In these words the principle of cosmic sociality—if we may so
express it—is contained. And the true human community is a
reflection of this cosmic principle. Here too it is important that the
community not group itself round an immobile center, but that the
center should be mobile, placed in the encircling round, moving
throughout it. The spiritual and moral depth of this location can be
recognized in the spirit of the words spoken by Christ Jesus in the
circle of the Twelve: 'Ye are my friend if ye do whatsoever I com-
mand you. Henceforth I call you not servants, for the servant
knoweth not what his lord doeth; but I have called you friends, for
all things that I have heard of my Father, I have made known unto
you.' (John xv:15)

These words contain the spiritual essence of the deep esoteric
conviction that must determine the forming of community, for they
reveal the *aim* of the highest model of all communities based on the

spirit, namely, that the group of disciples should become a circle of friends.

To work in this spirit becomes natural to a life of knowledge and cognition that has sunk deep into the heart; for it is one of the properties of the human heart to overcome the didactic, the pedagogic, and even the medical attitude to our fellows who work and strive alongside us, and in place of these attitudes substitute free intercourse and give-and-take based upon human confidence. This is the object of everyone's *desire*, whether conscious or unconscious. Though the desire cannot be fulfilled without further effort—and, generally a very prolonged quest—yet faith in such a possibility is tenacious and refuses to be dislodged. It is tenacious because behind the desire for a purely human structure of community life there exists an unconscious knowledge that the supersensible organization of the human heart bears within itself the power of interchanging the fruits of learning, education, and healing with different and more direct methods than those of instruction, precept, and prescription. For the organization of the human heart makes it possible *for one human being to live in another.*

And this does not come about merely by personal sympathy, but by real interest in the other's *problems.* For if the problems of knowledge have become concerns of the heart, interest in one another's problems of knowledge will also become a concern of the heart; and that is the necessary condition for a human circle whose center lies in its circumference. It can then live in this encircling round—in such a way that, in rhythmic succession, every point thereof becomes, at a definite time, a decisive and determining center. In practice this means that at a definite point of time and in a definite situation each member of a human circle striving after spiritual knowledge has to be, for the moment, its center of gravity, bearing the weight of responsibility for the whole, though it may be only by a determining word or by a single decisive act. No one in the present age can alone be permanently responsible for a circle of men and women pursuing the spiritual life of knowledge, but everyone who belongs to such a circle will at some point of time and in some definite situation be alone responsible—for at that moment the decision lies in *his or her* hands.

To be ready for the decision that lays its claim on *every* member of a spiritual knowledge-community, *spirit-awareness* is as necessary as is *spirit-beholding* for the realization of individual freedom. Practice of spirit-awareness makes us aware of the responsibility of the moment in respect of the whole work we are sharing in community with others. The second verse of the Foundation Stone has this meaning *also*, as the foundation stone of social cooperation in a community pursuing the life of spiritual knowledge.

> *Human Soul!*
> Thou livest in the beat of heart and lung
> Which leads thee through the Rhythm of Time
> Into the realm of thine own soul's feeling.
> Practice *Spirit Awareness*
> In balance of the soul,
> Where the Surging Deeds
> of the World's Becoming
> Thine own I
> Unite with the World I.
> And thou wilt truly *feel*
> In Human Soul Weaving.

In this verse is contained the secret as well as the strength of the *principle of spiritual community*, expressed in the gospel text: 'Where two or three are gathered together in my name, there am I in the midst of them.'

3

THE FATHER-FOUNDATION
OF ALL HUMANKIND

IN ITS OPERATION on the inner life, the third verse of the Foundation Stone has among other things the task of overcoming a misunderstanding that is often deeply rooted. It is the mistake of regarding spiritual science itself as an *object of knowledge,* whereas in reality the *universe* is the object, for the knowledge of which spiritual science is the means. Spiritual science is not there to be an object of knowledge, but to help us attain direct knowledge of the world. An inner orientation toward and an understanding of this *direct knowledge* flows from the words:

Human Soul!
Thou livest in the resting head
Which from the Grounds of Eternity
Opens to thee the World Thoughts.
Practice S*pirit Beholding*

These words exhort us to direct our faculty of penetrating vision to the Spirit reigning in the *world,* which sets free the cosmic thoughts from the Spirit's eternal grounds of Being.

Yet even this direct knowledge is not an end in itself, for in the long run the point is not that the individual should be enriched by knowledge but should be a *mediator* passing on the knowledge to others who need it equally. The point is not that one or another should attain to freedom by knowledge of the truth, but that we should form a link in the chain of humanity's liberation through knowledge of the truth. To the impulse of knowledge, the social impulse must be added; the life of knowledge has a community-forming task. This is why the Christ-verse of the Foundation Stone precedes the Spirit-verse—as it does also spiritually and morally. The Christ verse points to the necessity of the social principle, in order to change death into life.

Here again there may be misunderstanding, for a community of human beings must not be regarded as the final *object* of the fruitful and health-bringing life of knowledge they pursue. Such a community is once again only a mediator by whose help service is done to all humankind. Just as the *universe*, and not the science of it, is the object of our knowledge, so, in a group or society that pursues this knowledge, the object is not the group or society itself, but *humankind*. Misunderstanding will best be overcome in the spirit of the *first* verse of the Foundation Stone, for this verse contains the impulse to universality, a universality that exposes all cliquishness, insularity, and narrowness as jarring discord and bad taste. The Father-verse of the Foundation Stone directs the soul to the universal being of all humanity. *This* is the *third* aspect of our Foundation Stone—that it is essential for those who wish to belong to the anthroposophical movement that their souls be thus attuned—no less essential than that they understand and feel the principle of individual freedom and that of community.

It is of course not a mere matter of external behavior, but a fundamental perception that of itself produces the corresponding attitude of soul. The condition demanded is contained in the words 'practice spirit-recollection' and the result of fulfilling it is the 'and thou wilt truly live' spoken of in the same verse. '*True will*' is the end product of the living realization that all humanity 'is born from the Divine'.

If the truth of the statement 'From the Divine humanity is born' is rightly understood, it sets the will free from the narrowing influences of country, nationality, and race, raising it to the stage of pure humanity, permeated by the cosmos. To be purely and simply human is an expression of the deep consciousness that we are not born *from* blood and soil, but are on the contrary born as strangers *into* the blood and the soil, originating from the Father-spirit of the Heights in common with all humankind.

The only true fatherland of the real human being is the land common to all humanity, that of the eternal Father in the Heavens. And if we fail to discern this fact by means of free spiritual insight—by means of spirit-recollection—we will yet be *compelled* to acknowledge it by the destiny of all humanity—the primordial law of the Father—namely, the necessity of toil (work), suffering (sickness), and death. The iron bands of toil, suffering, and death maintain the destined unity of humankind even when certain sections of it—through arrogance or fear—endeavor to conceal, forget, or obliterate from consciousness the fact of universal kinship.

If we can be awakened in no other way to the memory of our common origin and kinship, there still remain the pangs of childbirth, the sweat of toil, and the agony of the death-bed—reminders warning us never to feel so much at home on earth as to forget entirely our heavenly origin. Yet those who belong to the movement founded by Rudolf Steiner should also acquire and maintain the consciousness of their origin by the *direct* path of spirit-recollection, following the precepts of the verse beginning:

Human Soul!
Thou livest in the limbs
Which bear thee through the World of Space
Into the Spirit's Ocean Being.
Practice *Spirit Recollection*
In depths of soul,
Where in the Wielding Will
of World Creating
Thine own I
Comes to being in God's I.
And thou wilt truly *live*
In Human World Being.

The same reality—whereof toil, suffering, and death warn humanity with compelling force—shall be recognized and experienced by means of a free inward striving by those in touch with the movement founded by Rudolf Steiner. This knowledge will immerse the soul in a spiritual and moral current of universality, so that the narrowing influences of blood and country[1] will gradually lose their significance in face of the greatness and tragedy of that which now comes into consciousness—*the destiny of all humankind in the world.*

1. Valentin Tomberg is referring here to the Nazi movement rooted in a false consciousness of the 'pure blood' of the Aryan people and their 'right to land' (country) to express themselves. Tomberg clearly foresaw that the precepts 'Blut und Boden' ('blood and country') of the Nazis would lead to tragedy, which indeed ensued with tragic necessity in the shape of World War II.

4

THE TASK OF SPIRITUAL
SCIENCE IN THE WORLD

IN THE LAST SECTION it was pointed out that a community in which spiritual knowledge is pursued does not exist for its own sake but for the sake of humanity. It is only justified when it proves itself of *real* service to humanity and the world. In this connection therefore it may be asked how humanity and the world have been served by the community founded at Christmas 1923, whose spiritual Foundation Stone we are considering. And from this follows the question: What actually is the mission of spiritual science to the world?

The society Rudolf Steiner founded in 1923 was planned according to the deep sense of the mission expressed in the Foundation Stone. We may summarize in three words all that has been said concerning the three verses of the Foundation Stone. The three words are: *universal anthroposophical society*. In these three words the whole content of the three verses is included: universality, through spirit-recollection of the Father; community (society), through spirit-awareness of the Son; and spiritual science, namely wisdom (sophia) freely received by the human being (anthropos) in spirit-beholding. Those who plunge their soul deeply enough into the Foundation Stone will find that the words 'universal anthroposophical society' can in themselves be significant material for meditation—so much the more effective, as they contain an immense number of spiritual facts, condensed into a living force. In this society itself the purpose was to pour this triune force into humanity and the world—to be an instrument for the radiation of this force.

Since then, however, much has changed, and the main question now relates to the mission of spiritual science in general, for humanity, and the world.

The tragedy of the nineteenth century consisted chiefly in the fact that two worlds—the earthly and the spiritual—confronted each other in silence: the concepts evolved by human beings on earth were mute for the spiritual world; the speech of the spiritual world, woven of ethical and spiritual tones, was mute for the apprehension of earthly humanity. The spiritual world could *work* into the earthly world at that time, but could not *speak* to it. Then came Rudolf Steiner, who created a new *language*, one that not only could be understood on earth in thoughts and concepts, but could also be morally heard in the spiritual world. By means of this language the gulf separating the two worlds has been bridged. Through this new language more and more truths *can* now flow from the spiritual world, while ever more and more the tidings of our human needs and problems rise to the spiritual world. The union of the two worlds *is* consummated: spiritual science has fulfilled *this* part of its mission in the world.

Yet this attainment is only part of the mission of spiritual science in the world. Something more must follow: there must be a gradual metamorphosis of the human *word* (comprising the human faculties of thought and speech). In the present age the human word is still only an imparter of thoughts and ideas. It speaks *of* what is good, but cannot of itself impart goodness. The change that must take place in the human word consists in thought absorbing in itself not only what is right and true, but the essential substance of the good. Then will the word be the bearer, not of meaning alone, but of meaning kindled with moral fire.

This metamorphosis of the word, to become the bearer of the moral element, is possible because by means of spiritual science a new logic will be learned and applied. The merely formal logic of dialectical accuracy will merge into a logic filled with being—the logic of true moral greatness. This process corresponds to the harmony of heart and head in the human organism. The union of the greatest clarity of thought with the highest moral tone of which the heart is capable will in the future possess the convincing force attributed nowadays to a 'proof'. The word itself, founded in the heart and directed by the head, will become *good*, that is to say its effect will be morally enriching, even as uttered thoughts enrich the body of knowledge in our day. In future the word will possess elemental force, and yet that force will be of pure morality. The *moral ether* will first reveal itself through human beings in the moral efficacy of the human word.

This will require certain drastic changes in the whole human organism, and these changes form the further mission of spiritual science to humanity. This future mission of spiritual science is expressed in the *fourth* verse of the Foundation Stone.

At the turning point of time
The Spirit Light of the World
Entered the Stream of Earthly Being.
Darkness of Night had held its sway.
Day-radiant Light streamed into human souls:
Light that gives warmth
To simple Shepherds' Hearts.
Light that enlightens
The wise Heads of Kings.

O Light Divine,
O Sun of Christ,
Warm Thou our hearts,
Enlighten Thou our heads,
That Good may become —
What from our hearts we found
And from our heads direct
With single purpose.

The concluding words, 'That Good may become—/What from our hearts we found/And from our heads direct/With single purpose,' contain the aspiration for the union of head and heart that can produce the *Good that may become* of what goes out from human beings into the world. The first thing destined to be *good* in the deeper sense of spiritual science is the most human thing of all that we pour out into the world—namely, *the word.*

Spiritual science is in the world not only to create a new language in the vertical direction between earth and heaven—this, as we saw, it has already done—but to create a new language on the horizontal plane from person to person. The *scepticism* that denies the possibility of intercourse between earth and heaven militates against this task, and so does the *hatred* that divides humanity into dumbly antagonistic groups. Thus it happens that in many places and by many individuals, spiritual science is today, in the literal sense, being crucified: the cross, formed out of scepticism and hatred, condemns it to mute ineffectiveness. It is effective however wherever it is accepted as a living *language* that on the one hand opens up approaches to ever-growing knowledge and on the other helps us to such a deep and honest mutual understanding as could never be attained without it.

The Foundation Stone expresses the *fundamental* impulse of spiritual science; but even more, it not only expresses, but *contains* this impulse. And as it is intended for *meditation*, it has the virtue also of awakening and strengthening this basic impulse when we work with it meditatively. Work with this meditation will awaken in the soul of everyone who labors honestly the force of faith in spiritual science, making possible true intercourse between the human being and the spiritual world—and also intercourse, humanly worthy and noble, between individuals.

PART 3

THE FOUNDATION STONE MEDITATION
AS REVELATION OF THE TRUE RELATIONSHIP
BETWEEN MAN AND NATURE

FOREWORD

THE FOLLOWING PAGES conclude the author's studies on Rudolf Steiner's Foundation Stone. This last study has been developed to the same depth and extent as the two preceding ones. The first was concerned with the relationship of the human being to the divine-spiritual world, and the second was concerned with the nature of human community. This last one is devoted to the relationship of human beings to the kingdoms of nature. The reader should therefore consider this work as concluded in the sense that, by means of the Foundation Stone, illumination is gained regarding the age-old question of the being of and relationship between what are summarized in the traditional 'simple' words 'God, Man, and Nature'.[1]

As with the two preceding studies, this short work is intended for those who not only have the text of the Foundation Stone but also want to make spiritual-moral use of it.

VALENTIN TOMBERG, ROTTERDAM, 1939.

---

1. In this study the word 'Man' embraces Man and Woman in the sense of the words of Genesis: 'So the Elohim created Man in their own image, in the image of the Elohim they created him; male and female they created them.' (Gen. 1:27)

INTRODUCTION

GEORGE ADAMS

VALENTIN TOMBERG is the author of some of the most remarkable works which the Anthroposophical movement has produced. . . . His writings on the Foundation Stone Mediation . . . give a peculiarly direct and deep feeling of the reality and presence of the spiritual world and spiritual beings. He treats the meditation as a gateway *through* which the soul can be brought to a realization of the spiritual world, and above all, of man's own grounding in the spiritual world, in relation to the Divine Father, the Son, and the Holy Spirit. He finds the working of the Nine Hierarchies quite severally and specifically expressed in the words which Rudolf Steiner uttered on that memorable occasion. Those who are able to read Tomberg's writings will find in them much stimulus and inspiration.[1]

GEORGE ADAMS

---

1. 'Friends Old and New', from *The Anthroposophical Movement*, vol. xiv, no. 7, July 7, 1937.

1

THE 'STONE' OF THE
FOUNDATION STONE MEDITATION

NATURE, WITH HER THREE KINGDOMS spread out before us, presents a vast perceptible picture that calls upon us to make it complete with an embracing concept that arises through us. For in the
sense of Rudolf Steiner's *Philosophy of Freedom,* no percept without
its corresponding *concept* is a reality: it becomes reality only when
what presents itself as appearance to the powers of perception is
grasped by the capacity to form concepts. This applies also to that
all-embracing percept designated as 'nature'. In itself, the percept is
not reality so long as the other half—namely, the conceptual—is not
added to it. A concept must be added, one that encompasses in itself
all the particulars of nature's existence. This concept should be such
that, in it, all substances, forces, and beings within the kingdoms of
nature might be comprised in a way that is not word-bound and
abstract, but that accords with reality and is concrete. This concept
of nature need not actually be found, however, for it is *already at
hand.* And indeed, it is not at hand as an abstract, logical formula,
but as a concrete living reality in the world. This concept relating
to nature, and comprising her, is present as the creation of divine
logic. One may for example regard the first chapter of Genesis from
this point of view. There one may indeed come to see why, after
warmth, air, water, and the firmament were created and inhabited
by plants 'according to their kind' and by animals of the air, water,
and earth 'according to their kind', the following expression of
divine logic is found: 'Let us make Man in our image and after our
own likeness; and let him have dominion over the fish of the sea, and
over the fowl of the air, and over the cattle, and over all the earth,
and over every creeping thing that creepeth upon the earth.' For

Man is the 'concept' of nature, embracing in itself all the kingdoms and beings of nature in a higher unity. The biblical 'to have dominion over' is in fact not to be understood as possessing power, but as 'an encompassing and self-comprehending representing' of nature by Man. For Man is the comprising of the kingdoms and beings of nature in a conscious unity: Man is the living 'concept' created by the gods[1] of the living percept 'nature', and is therefore also the *meaning* of nature: in the same way as letters that do not express a word have no meaning, so would nature have no meaning were she not to let herself be 'expressed' through Man. And indeed, she does 'speak' through Man in such a way that the separate members of Man's being encompass her separate kingdoms. For example, if the human ether body were to lose the force that holds it together and thus fall apart, the whole *animal kingdom* would arise out of the pieces of this 'exploded' ether body.[2] Were the same to happen with the human astral body, the whole plant world would come into manifestation out of its fragments. And an explosion of the 'I' would bring the whole mineral kingdom into appearance once again. This fact, to which Rudolf Steiner has referred, means however that the human ether body is the 'concept' of the percept 'animal kingdom', and that the human astral body and the human 'I' are the 'concepts' of the plant and mineral kingdoms.

This is nothing other than to have expressed in spiritual-scientific conceptual form what is expressed pictorially in Genesis in the words: 'Let us make Man in our image, after our likeness: and let him have dominion over the fish of the sea, and over the fowl of the air, and over the cattle, and over all the earth, and over every creeping thing that creepeth upon the earth.' (Gen. 1:26)

Now the fact that Man is the concept of nature has the added meaning that human beings comprise within themselves the total responsibility for these kingdoms of nature. Human beings thereby

---

1. The expression 'gods' refers to the beings of the spiritual hierarchies, such as the Elohim—'So the Elohim created Man in their own image, in the image of the Elohim they created him; male and female they created them.' (Gen. 1:27)

2. Cf. Rudolf Steiner's *Gegenwärtiges und Vergangenes im Menschengeiste* [GA 167], Berlin, 1916, lecture seven (not yet translated into English).

cease to regard themselves—as happens so often—as their own 'private affairs': if they regard themselves as the representative of the whole of nature to the spiritual world, they will come to the moral insight that they must also stand as representatives for the spiritual world to nature. For in standing for nature, they also stand for nature's destiny; that is, they are responsible for nature's fortune and misfortune. Her fortune and misfortune are however dependent on whether she is connected with the spiritual world or separated from it. She can only be connected with the spiritual world through *Man*; she does not possess her *own* connection. Man is the sole connecting link between nature and the spiritual world, for the consciousness of nature runs in the *horizontal*, whereas human consciousness is capable of establishing the *vertical* connection with the spiritual world. If human beings do this, they take part in the life of nature as well as in the working of the spiritual world. As 'concept' of nature, human beings comprise in themselves the three kingdoms of nature—as 'image' and 'likeness' of the gods, they take in the thinking, feeling, and willing of the gods. And indeed, it is in this way that Man elevates the 'concept' of nature vertically to the spiritual world, where the 'concept' of the lowest becomes the highest. That is, in their 'I's, human beings stand for the mineral kingdom with respect to the spiritual world, in their astral bodies for the plant kingdom, and in their ether bodies for the animal kingdom; their own human kingdom they represent to the spiritual world through their physical bodies.

On the other hand, in the horizontal direction—that is, in their relationship to nature—human beings are connected with nature in such a way that their physical bodies carry the mineral kingdom in itself, their ether bodies comprise the life forces of the plant kingdom in itself, and their astral bodies are connected with the animal world.

The following schematic diagram gives the relationship of Man 'uniting heaven and earth' to the kingdoms of nature: 'natural' Man's relationship in the horizontal, as well as 'spiritual' Man's in the vertical.[3]

3. The attentive reader of spiritual-scientific literature will find here the solution to one of the many apparent 'contradictions' that so often appear in the works

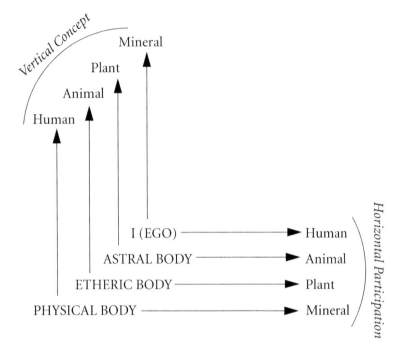

The vertical line of this diagram is the line of the 'concepts' of the kingdoms of nature raising themselves, in Man, to the spiritual world, while the horizontal line denotes Man's 'participation' in nature, that is, relationship to her as *a being of nature*. From this we can also grasp, for example, that on the one hand human beings *take into themselves* the mineral substances in order to build up the physical body, and on the other constitute, in the 'I', the *concept* of the mineral world for the spiritual world. On this basis, the human '*I*' has been spoken of as the *true stone* from far back in time; the Apocalypse describes it as the 'white stone, with a new name written on the stone, which no one knows except him who receives it.' (Rev. 2:17)

---

and lectures of Rudolf Steiner. Here the contradiction in question is that which seems to arise from Rudolf Steiner's statements regarding the relationship of the human being to the kingdoms of nature, such as are found, for example, in the cycle *Gegenwärtiges und Vergangenes im Menschengeiste* (see preceding note) and in the book *An Outline of Esoteric Science* (chap. 2).

In the Middle Ages, a specific lofty stage of 'I'-development was spoken of as the 'Philosopher's Stone'. In Valentin Andreas' work *The Chymical Wedding of Christian Rosenkreutz*, the stage of the 'I' 'become sun-like' is described as the 'Knighthood of the Golden Stone'.[4]

Further, Rudolf Steiner designates the condition of the human 'I' striven for in the spiritual-scientific movement as 'the stone that, in the form of the dodecahedron,' must now be present in the souls of human beings who represent this movement. This 'stone' is the *foundation stone* of the movement, and the Foundation Stone meditation is the means through which and with which the Foundation Stone as such may be built up and experienced.

4. Op. cit., 7th lecture.

2

THE DODECAHEDRAL STONE
AS MAN'S TASK AND AS HOPE
OF THE MINERAL WORLD

IF FOR EXAMPLE one decides to practice the meditation on the Rose-Cross as described in *An Outline of Esoteric Science*,[1] then in a relatively short time, in order to arrive at the three stages of that exercise, one will also experience definite difficulties. Indeed, one may experience that the first stage—that of concentration on the self-created symbol of the Rose-Cross—demands the overcoming of the inclination to wander about in one's thoughts and representations. With the second step, however—namely, where what matters is extinguishing the self-constructed symbol and concentrating only on the pictureless aspect of what one's own soul has experienced while building up and absorbing itself in the picture symbol—one is concerned not only with a wandering imaginative life, but also with a dulling of consciousness that sets in. And then again, should the conditions for the third stage of the meditation be fulfilled—that is, if one then extinguishes the experiences of the soul in an effort to attain a completely object-free state of consciousness—then what is experienced is above all the incapacity of consciousness to give itself any kind of stimulus when the supports of perceptions, thoughts, pictures, and feeling experiences are abandoned. For what matters here is to inwardly create a content out of oneself, through oneself, and in oneself that is independent of memories, pictures, thoughts, and feelings. This incapacity is however experienced not only as a

1. Anthroposophic Press, 1997 [GA 13].

dulling of consciousness but above all as *numbness*: this consciousness is initially experienced as being as incapable of motion as is a
petrified stone. In the second stage of the exercise the dullness one
encounters is experienced, however, as a kind of 'vegetating' of consciousness. And the wandering about with which one has had to
struggle in the first stage is best compared to the animal soul condition, which is driven by instinct. Just as the animal is impelled to
movement from the depths of the unconscious, so too does the difficulty in concentration lie in an impelling restlessness, or a slacken-
ing-off of the inner life—ushering in sleep.

Thus, relatively early, certain experiences are encountered
through means of sincere efforts at meditation. Human beings initially experience themselves as simply *human*, with all the supports
the physical body alone affords them. On arising into the ether
body—at the first stage of the meditation—they become somewhat
more passive, as passive as is an animal in its consciousness compared to a human. Further, on entering into the experience of the
astral body—which corresponds to the second stage of the meditation—they find that they become one stage more passive in their
consciousness; indeed, as much more passive as is a plant compared
to an animal. And should they attempt to experience themselves in
the 'I', free of the whole threefold bodily organization—in the third
stage of the meditation—they find that their consciousness becomes
numb, as numb as is an immobile, rigid mineral.

The meditator can now say 'I possess a certain measure of forces.
They are sufficient for experiencing myself with full consciousness
in the physical body as a human being. However, for experiencing
myself with the same clarity of consciousness in the higher members of my being, they do not suffice. I must acquire them specifically by practice. My endeavours in meditation are indeed to serve
this end.' Such an approach is thoroughly sensible and justified. But
it is unsatisfactory to the degree that it remains content with a relatively superficial answer regarding the reason for this incapacity of
human consciousness to experience itself in full clarity in the higher
members of its being. A lack of forces is still no *real* reason, since it
must also have its cause. If human beings are a part of cosmic
existence—which they are, as microcosm—then all the forces of the

macrocosm should be present in them; and if certain forces are lacking, then the question ought to be *why* are they lacking? Asking this question brings us to the point where we can judge the inclination of consciousness to wander, its dullness, and its numbness, not only from an *absence* of forces (still to be attained) but also from the point of view of the *presence* of other forces hindering progress. We see more and more through our own experience that the apparent 'lack' of strength in consciousness is brought about by the working of forces of a moral nature. For example, the condition of numbness of consciousness is not natural, but is the consequence of the effect of a power. This power confronts spiritual students during their efforts to go further into their inner being. But they meet it also in the outer world. In the inner world they meet the power of numbness if they wish to reach the stage of the exercise leading to intuition. In the outer world they recognize it again in the condition in which the whole world of *mineral nature* finds itself. And so one of the first results of intuition is the significant objective intuitive insight that the same power of numbness acts both in humankind's inner being and in the whole kingdom of mineral nature. Thus the world of mineral nature appears as bound, numb will—the will that once streamed forth from the Spirits of Will, the Thrones, during the Old Saturn stage of development, and that was originally wholly active warmth.

In Rudolf Steiner's *An Outline of Esoteric Science* there is a short characterization of the fifth stage of the Rosicrucian path of knowledge,[2] which concerns the stage of becoming conscious of the correspondences between the microcosm and the macrocosm. Now these correspondences are not recognized simply by asking, for example, to what in the macrocosm my liver corresponds. Rather, one advances through striving towards intuitive knowledge and so finding oneself facing *cosmic-moral responsibilities*. For example, the still elementary knowledge of the real power of numbness in humankind's inner being leads further to the knowledge of its task[3] with respect to the power of numbness working in the macrocosm.

2. Op. cit., pp 371–373.
3. Ibid, p393.

One recognizes that, in our inner life, this power which holds the whole of mineral nature under the spell of numbness must be vanquished.

And so the 'connection' between the microcosm and the macrocosm is realized not just as a connection in thought, but in the *will*: the task and responsibility of the human will towards the world. In general, this is how one arrives at all real knowledge of the 'connection of microcosm and macrocosm': in humankind a new level of the sleeping will awakens and then becomes aware of a moral duty to the world at large.

In this way one also arrives, through the understanding of the inner power of numbness, at a more definite understanding of a 'connection between the microcosm and macrocosm'. One awakens in one's consciousness to our task of releasing the mineral kingdom from the spell of numbness. If this spell is overcome in us, to whom the destiny of nature has been entrusted, this overcoming then extends further along karmic paths throughout nature. In *An Outline of Esoteric Science* Rudolf Steiner puts it succinctly: 'Then, after an intermediate stage, which presents itself as a sojourn in a higher world, the Earth will transform itself into the Jupiter state. Within this state, what is now called the mineral kingdom will no longer exist; the forces of this mineral kingdom will be transmuted into plant forces. The plant kingdom, which in contrast to the present plant kingdom will have an entirely new form, appears during the Jupiter state as the lowest kingdom.'[4] This quotation, then, contains not only a world of facts, but also humanity's first cosmic task (that is, knowledge of the 'connection between microcosm and macrocosm'), namely to bring about, through the overcoming of the power of numbness in our own inner being, the release of the mineral kingdom from the spell of that same power.

What is the 'overcoming of the power of numbness in humanity's inner being'? What should the human 'I' be like in order to become capable of this? From a 'stone' that is grounded in the physical body, the ether body, and the astral body, and that rests in itself (that is,

4. Ibid.,

from a 'cube' that is defined by four sides),[5] the human 'I' must become a living, active 'stone', a *totally awakened will*, presenting a focal point for the twelve cosmic forces.[6] The resting 'cube' should become a shining 'dodecahedron'—this is the spiritually-real formula for the 'how' and 'what' of the overcoming of numbness in the human 'I'. It indicates the task that the 'I' become spiritually and morally awake to the impulses of the Father, the Son, and the Holy Spirit within each of the aspects, body, soul, spirit, and personality. These twelve 'directions' for the awakening of the 'I' are contained in Rudolf Steiner's Foundation Stone. This meditation consists of four verses, of which one each is dedicated to the four basic impulses of good: to the Father, the Son, the Spirit, and the Persona (Christ *after* he had become Jesus Christ). At the same time each relates to body, soul, and spirit. In this sense the Foundation Stone is contained in the form of a 'dodecahedron'. The meditation has the significance of fashioning a 'dodecahedron' from the 'cube' of the human 'I'; that is, of furthering it in the direction of the future Jupiter evolution. Herewith, however, work on the Foundation Stone signifies not only development of the self in the sense of one's own being, but also and expressly, working in the direction of freeing the mineral world from the misfortune of numbness.

---

5. Properly speaking a cube has *six* square faces, each comprising *four* sides. The author has apparently chosen to correlate these four sides to the quaternary nature of the human being (physical body, ether body, astral body, and the 'I') while retaining the three-dimensionality of the cube as a means to bring it into connection with the three-dimensional, twelve-sided figure of the dodecahedron. [ED]

6. The twelve instreaming cosmic forces of the zodiac. [ED]

3

THE WORK ON THE DODECAHEDRAL STONE AND THE FUTURE REDEMPTION OF MINERAL NATURE

SINCE EARLY TIMES occultism has spoken of three dangers to which the spiritual student can fall victim: *spiritual egoism*, *spiritual pessimism* (which leads to materialism), and *fatalism*. These dangers threatening especially those who have entered into spiritual training arise out of the tendency of the human soul to one-sidedness—that is, out of the tendency to satisfy its quest with the acquired viewpoint of *one side* of the world and to rest content with that. So it can happen, for example, that one experiences the reality of the spirit in the soul and as a result begins to think that what matters in life is to have this experience as often and for as long as possible. The consequence of this, however, is that one gradually proceeds from love of the spirit as the light of truth to love of the enjoyment of this spirit. An egoism is thereby fostered that is much more dangerous than the egoism of ordinary human life. For the latter is constantly corrected by life itself and kept within bounds. One cannot, for example, be a total egoist in life and carry out the obligations of a profession as well. It is different with the 'spiritual egoism' that can arise in the way indicated above, for it is not corrected by anything and can grow unbounded into the infinite, for only duties and tasks the soul gives itself count in this realm. With no challenge of selflessness, there are also no limits to the growth of egoism, that is to say to the tendency 'to cultivate the inner life' in forgetfulness of all humankind's misfortunes and tasks. Misfortune and want may loudly proclaim themselves all around, but the soul that has engrossed itself in the 'cultivation of the inner life' will be deaf to them. The one-sided and exclusive emphasis of the *Spirit* becomes in this way egoistic mysticism.

One-sided and exclusive emphasis on the *Son* can become a source of another danger. It can lead the soul to the point where it says to itself: whether one knows much or little is not the essential thing. The essential thing is to be good. All too often in life those who know much are not actually 'better' than those who know little. Indeed, the opposite is often experienced. Ignorant 'simple' souls often possess good qualities to a higher degree than those full of spiritual-scientific thoughts and viewpoints. Through such thinking the soul can come to the point where it becomes accustomed to regard morality (goodness) as independent of a world outlook. It is only one step further to arrive at an 'ideology-free morality', first in outlook and then in practice. In the end, the soul's conviction will be that only deeds matter—and as the actual realm of deeds is the physical world, it is this world alone, then, that matters. So the pessimistic relationship to the pure life of knowledge becomes an ideology-free morality, which in practice then leads to the neglect of the spiritual world, that is, to *materialism.*

One-sided and exclusive focus of the soul upon the *Father* principle fosters the habit in the soul of constantly experiencing a higher power working into the world from above. This then leads the soul to gradually accustom itself to ascribing responsibility for everything that happens—and also that *does not* happen—to this power alone. It gradually loses consciousness of its own responsibility for bringing about events of destiny. The more it recognizes an 'omnipotence', the stronger becomes its own *impotence*, which in the sphere of morality becomes lack of responsibility, and as a world-conception can be designated as *fatalism.*

So the one-sided fixating tendency in the human soul to become set in *one* direction in its relation to the Spirit, the Son, and the Father leads to errors with serious consequences. Moreover, when in time it advances to the stage of working right into the ether body, it leads to illness, to a pathological soul condition.

What has been said here in connection with the most essential principles of the spiritual moral life is also fundamentally valid for *all* outlooks one can have on life and death, destiny, and history. Each idea, however true and exalted, that does not present a bridge to another idea and remains standing over time as something definitive in itself, becomes of necessity an *idée fixe*. First it leads to monotony in our way of seeing things; then to lack of interest in other ideas and points of view; then to intolerance and moral narrow-mindedness; and finally to the pathological state of a fixed idea. In this way, for example, Friedrich Nietzsche's idea of the 'will-to-power' was already close to the border of the pathological state of a fixed idea. The wish to explain all phenomena of the spiritual and moral life through the 'will-to-power'—without taking into account at least another eleven different points of view—is in itself a pathological state (even though a subtle and 'unrecognized' one). Similarly, the way of looking at human soul life introduced by Sigmund Freud can be regarded as approaching a pathological condition: the wish to explain *all* soul phenomena through sexuality bears the hallmarks of a fixed idea.

In this sense every outlook, every idea, can become illness if it is neither deepened with regard to content nor comprehended as one idea joined together with a world of *other* ideas. In this way, rigidly adhering to the gospel saying that 'None is good, but God alone' can lead first to modesty, but can then bring about a kind of 'inferiority complex' in the soul's consciousness. On the other hand, the contrasting gospel saying, 'Be ye perfect as your Father in heaven is perfect,' can first bring about courage, but then call forth a kind of 'megalomania' in the soul's consciousness. Yet when these *two* contrasting truths live in the consciousness at the same time or directly following one another, no danger exists in the sense of the effects of a fixed idea.

The spiritual background of this fact is the relationship of human consciousness to the zodiac. The twelve constellations of the fixed stars that form the zodiac are at the same time supersensible 'streams of revelation', each of which illuminates the world in a particular light. If we remain stationary for a long time in *one* 'sign' of the zodiac, the point of view, the way of seeing things that accords with this constellation then becomes a fixed idea. To avoid remaining stuck in a fixed idea, we must journey through the twelve constellations of the fixed stars in our consciousness: we must not fall victim to the numbing effect of the set fixed star constellations, but must maintain our inner mobility.

This inner mobility is none other than the power that overcomes the numbness initially experienced at the third stage of meditation. The numbness overcome in this way is the same force that in the cosmos brings about the numbness of the sense-perceptible starry world, and that also holds the mineral kingdom petrified on earth. When we are capable of moving through the circle of fundamental cosmic ideas, we overcome the numbing effect of the fixed star constellations and live with the spiritual revelation working through the zodiac. Two kinds of influence proceed from the zodiac: a numbing influence from the fixed stars, and a revealing one from the beings of the zodiac. We have to overcome the one, but open ourselves discerningly to the other by learning to move through the whole circle of the zodiac. To do this, we must learn to observe the world not from one point of view only, but from twelve points of view. Our 'I' must be capable of carrying out twelve different kinds of cognitive movement. If we have learned this, then the numbing power is overcome in our 'I'-consciousness, which then becomes a part of the world where the numbness controlling the starry world and the world of mineral nature is overcome. Here begins that process of overcoming, proceeding from the innermost part of the human being, that will ultimately call forth objective outer changes in nature, changes that will manifest during the future Jupiter existence. There will then no longer be a mineral kingdom in the sense of petrified and immobile substances.

The power of the 'I' to move from one outlook to another through the twelve signs of the zodiac was designated in antiquity as the power of 'belief', which was considered of a higher order than knowledge. If the process of cognition consists in attaining a certain outlook, then 'belief' transcends this in being able to pass from that outlook to *other* outlooks. It is the power of the 'I' to be a 'wanderer' through the circle of the modes of cognition. And it is this power of 'belief' that will release mineral nature in the future from the spell of immobility. Hence it is written in the gospel (Matt. 17:20) that with faith—even if only the size of a mustard-seed—it is possible to move mountains.

The first step toward the fulfilment of humankind's mission of redemption with respect to the petrified kingdoms of mineral nature is the overcoming of numbness in one's own consciousness: the 'stone' must become a dodecahedron in which all twelve streams of the cosmos are present and working together. And it was in order to initiate this first step that Rudolf Steiner gave the Foundation Stone. The Foundation Stone is so constituted as to not only guard against the dangers of one-sidedness and the fixed idea, but to prevail upon the human soul to contemplate and experience existence from *twelve points of view*. It contains in concentrated form the path of 'journeying through the circle of the twelve'. Its four verses each contain the bodily, soul, and cosmic-spiritual aspects of the *four* fundamental principles of the world. Thus, in the *first* verse the theme is the Father-principle, which manifests itself by way of the First Hierarchy in the limb-system through the spirit-recollection of the soul. In the *second* verse it is the Son-principle that is experienced through the activity of the Second Hierarchy in the rhythmic system through the spirit-awareness of the soul. And the *third* verse brings to expression the Spirit-principle as the awakening effect of the Third Hierarchy in the head through spirit-beholding of the soul. However, the divinity of the world is not exhausted with the Father, the Son, and the Holy Spirit, for these three eternal beings of the Godhead work to bring about a *fourth* in the world. For, as Old Saturn was the stage of the world's becoming that stood specifically in the sign of the Father—and as Old Sun and Old Moon signified especially the workings of the Son and the Spirit that followed on the working of the Father—so the *fourth* stage of evolution, the actual Earth evolution, signifies the arising of a *fourth* being of the *Eternal Good*. The Rosicrucians undoubtedly knew of this cosmic secret, and for this reason they often represented the Eternal Good as a *fourfoldness* in their symbols and figures, where, next to the Father, the Son, and the Holy Spirit, the 'Persona' or 'Jesus Christ' was mentioned. In the 'Persona' (Personality) they beheld the fourth principle of the Good, that is to say the new element of *this* Earth evolution in relation to the three preceding stages. For them, Jesus Christ, through his having been crucified and resurrected, was something new in the world. No longer was he simply the Son, nor yet simply the Christ-being, who was known as the Cosmic Sun-being in olden times—he was none other than *Jesus Christ*, the archetype and prototype of the personality who had in Himself united into one the divine and the human. This unity, which the Rosicrucians designated as the 'Persona', is the ideal—the *new* ideal of the world—which, as such, holds good both for the beings of the spiritual hierarchies and for humanity. To this fourth divinity in the world the *fourth* verse of the Foundation Stone is dedicated. There the threefold bodily organization is drawn together for deeds springing from the head and heart of the whole soul that has made the *personality* a vessel for the revelation of the totality of the spiritual hierarchies.

And so the actual practice of the Foundation Stone bears within it the practice of 'journeying through the twelve points of view' of the circle, which brings about the inner mobility of our 'I'. Through this the power of numbness is overcome first in our inner being, in order then—in ways delineated by karma—to overcome it in nature also, that is, to bring about the redemption of the mineral kingdom in the way it is to take place in the future Jupiter existence.

4

THE WORK ON THE
FUTURE REDEMPTION OF
THE PLANT WORLD

IN THE PRACTICE OF MEDITATION, the overcoming of *dullness* must precede the overcoming of numbness in consciousness. Dullness begins when the self-created image—for example, the image of the Rose-Cross—is extinguished, so that what remains as the object of consciousness is the soul's own activity that first formed the image. What remains is a wordless and imageless inner activity—a remembering to which nothing externally representable and akin to the sense world is attached. Consciousness is in this way freed from the world of the senses, but it first grows dull. This dullness should be as little regarded as a mere absence of forces that keep consciousness awake, as is numbness, in the third stage of meditation, understood as a mere absence of certain powers of consciousness. Just as the numbness is brought about through certain forces, so is the dullness of consciousness brought about through forces of a spiritual moral kind. They appear first in the soul as *lack of interest*: the consciousness slackens and succumbs to dullness because it finds nothing—even if only self-created colors and forms—that would spur it from outside into activity. It is initially incapable of interesting itself in such a colorless and formless content. Just as with numbness, which can lead ultimately to fixed ideas, there is also this lack of interest, not just in meditation but also generally in the spiritual-moral life of human beings. This becomes evident through the way we hear, which depends upon our manner of listening. For there are many kinds and many degrees of listening: interest and lack of interest determine the differences in listening. One person

65

discerns meaningful things in the babbling of a child, another hears nothing special in the remarks of a truly wise man. What distinguishes these two is the degree of interest they are capable of mustering in their attention. However, the ability to summon up a high degree of interest is dependent not only on the capacity for concentration but also on the moral power to overcome lack of interest itself. For this reason many things can remain hidden even to the most clear-sighted and gifted people if they lack this moral power, while many less gifted people can recognize that which completely eludes those who are 'more outstanding'. But what appears initially as sheer lack of interest and also of the capacity to *wonder* can in time become a kind of psychic illness—that of *apathy* towards all and sundry. Just as the forces of numbness that proceed from the outer fixed star constellations present the danger of fixed ideas, so do the forces of dullness that proceed from the planetary bodies present the danger of apathy. And just as overcoming numbness depends on the awakened spiritual forces of the *zodiac* in one's 'I' in order to combat the forces of numbness of the fixed star constellations, so overcoming dullness likewise depends upon awakening the forces of the *planetary spheres* in one's soul, in order to combat the forces of dullness of the planetary bodies. For the working of the visible planets is such that it is constantly trying to remain in the sub-conscious; that is, it does not wish to be raised into consciousness. And this operates in the sphere of consciousness as lack of interest. In contrast, the spiritual-moral forces of the planetary spheres[1] strive to overcome this lack of interest. These spiritual-moral forces flow within the soul as forces of the different kinds of wakeful interest.

The efforts to overcome dullness of consciousness do not have only a subjective significance for the human soul, for through human souls they are also part of the battle being fought out in the world. Here it is a question of the battle against those forces that, in

---

1. Rudolf Steiner gives the concept of the difference between the visible planets and the planetary spheres in Lecture 6 of the cycle *The Spiritual Beings in the Heavenly Bodies and the Kingdoms of Nature* (Helsinki, 1912), GA 136, Anthroposophic Press, 1992.

nature, hold the *plant kingdom* under the spell of dullness. For the same force that, by means of dullness, bars the possibility of conscious inspired consciousness in the human soul also brings about the dull 'vegetating' existence of plants. That humanity is so deaf to the call of the spiritual world, and that the plants are so powerless, so bound to the earth and unable to soar freely towards the sun—this has *one* cause in the world. And insight into this one cause gives rise to further knowledge of the relationship between macrocosm and microcosm; that is, it produces the moral-spiritual consciousness of humanity's responsibility towards the plant kingdom. This consciousness also reveals to us how the future redemption of the plant kingdom must take place. The plant kingdom should be released from its bound state during the Jupiter condition, and, further, be released from its dull state of existence during the Venus condition. 'The plant kingdom, which in contrast to the present plant kingdom will have an entirely new form, appears during the Jupiter state as the lowest kingdom.' 'The Venus evolution will be one in which the plant kingdom also will have disappeared; the lowest kingdom at that time will be the transformed animal kingdom.'[2] These statements by Rudolf Steiner not only point to facts regarding the future but signify also humanity's mission for their realization. For as regards the spiritual-moral consciousness of our responsibility towards the kingdoms of nature, it is not so important to know what the future will be like as it is to work so that the future takes shape for the salvation of beings. And in this sense Rudolf Steiner's words represent tasks of humankind for the future—namely, to bring about first the transformation and then the redemption of the plant kingdom.

Fulfilling these tasks again begins in our inner life. What matters is educating the human soul life and keeping it as mobile and awake to the totality of 'moral space', as was the case with the life of knowledge for fulfilling our task in connection with the mineral kingdom. This latter task has to do with the 'power of faith', that is, with the capacity to 'journey' through the twelve cognitive outlooks, whereas

2. *An Outline of Esoteric Science*, p394.

now it is a matter of the 'power of love', the capacity to have an ear 'for the seven basic moral tones (vowels)' of the world and to meet them with interest. These 'seven basic moral tones' of the world are at the same time the moral content of space: they are the 'fullness' (the *pleroma* of the Gnostics) that fills out the 'void' (*kenoma*) of space. Through them the *directions* 'East', 'West', 'North', and 'South' receive their spiritual-moral significance as spiritual streams giving content to space. And this content consists of that which can be denoted on the one hand as 'East', 'West', 'North', 'South', 'Center', 'Inner', and 'All'; and on the other be recognized as the basic spiritual-moral tones of the world that manifest themselves in the seven stages of Christ Jesus' Passion: the Washing of the Feet, the Scourging, the Crowning with Thorns, the Carrying of the Cross, the Crucifixion, the Entombment, and the Resurrection. For the seven stages of the Passion reveal seven spiritual-moral 'laws' or 'principles' that represent the secret of space. Thus, for example, the principle of 'Foot-washing' stands behind the direction Above-Below. Everything that bows down, that descends through spiritual-moral motives, belongs to the cosmic 'Foot-washing' stream. Indeed, all the interest a human soul can summon up for the lower beings of nature stands also in the sign of the Washing of the Feet, for it indicates an inner bowing down. In this sense, to each of the seven directions of spiritual space there corresponds a particular soul attitude that always indicates an overcoming of the corresponding lack of interest. The soul must learn to become 'void' seven times over, and to fill the void each time with an interest that is not stimulated externally but which the soul develops out of itself. These seven stages of becoming void, the stages of the *kenoma*, are the prerequisite for the seven stages of manifestation of the *pleroma*, or the 'fullness' of space. The soul must go through the dying away of egoistic interest and then be placed before a void, which it overcomes as a void by allowing a new selfless interest to arise out of itself. This, in brief, is the inner method and drama of knowledge acquired by Inspiration. It consists essentially in creating connecting links with various higher beings in all directions of space by way of spiritual streams that first become empty and are then morally filled. The strivings of the human soul to fulfill the demands of Inspired cognition do not bear only the significance that the soul arrives at knowledge, but also the significance that the soul collaborates in overcoming the binding dullness in the world, that is, in the work of redeeming the plant kingdom.

With respect to the activity of redeeming the plant kingdom, work on the Foundation Stone has the potential of a root from which much more can then grow. For the essential thing in its inner composition is not solely the twelvefold aspect of existence fundamental to it, but also the fact that it is built up from the dynamic working of the directions of space. Each of the four verses has a spatial-dynamic form that is fundamental to it. Thus in the first verse, the working direction of the spiritual root-force is stated in words expressing the fact of humanity being rooted in divinity.

For the Father Spirit
Of the Heights holds sway
In Depths of Worlds
Begetting Being

And what rings out from the heights finds its *echo* in the depths of the 'Spirit's Ocean Being'. So the spatial-moral form for the first verse is the following (figure 1):

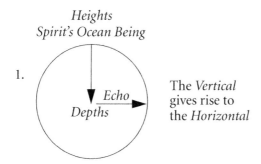

The second verse contains the form expressed by the words 'For the Christ Will in the encircling Round holds sway' and the 'Let there be fired from the East what in the West is formed.' (figure 2)

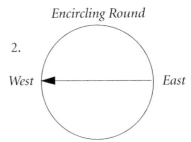

The third verse has as its realm of activity the sphere of the 'resting head,' and 'Let there be prayed from the Depths what in the Heights will be granted' gives the direction appropriate to it: (figure 3)

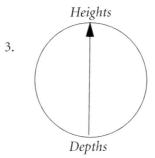

The fourth verse indicates the proceeding from within outward, which, through the union of head and heart, can become the point of outward radiation of the Christ impulse: that process of creativity in knowing and doing as presented and substantiated in detail in both parts of *The Philosophy of Freedom*,[3] the book on the divine nature of personality (as the *new* value in the world, which follows on the three eternal values). (figure 4)

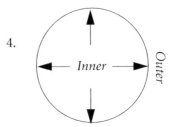

3. *Intuitive Thinking as a Spiritual Path* [GA 4].

If then one wishes to sum up the whole spiritual-spatial dynamic of the Foundation Stone, there arises the *cross*, and the *circle* that ultimately grows out of the middle point of the cross. This dynamic form overcomes the laming dullness of consciousness, which is brought about through lack of interest. If one is as unegoistic as a plant yet able to call forth interest as can only a human being with red blood, then the task of the form of the cross with the circle of roses that grow out of its mid-point is realized. The Rose-Cross arises out of the Foundation Stone, no longer as the 'Foundation Stone in dodecahedral form' for the life of knowledge, but now as the seven-fold archetype for the *moral growth* of the soul. And if we learn to raise up and activate this moral growth right into the bright clarity of our consciousness, we also bring it about that the growth of the plant world will pass over more and more into the realm of laws belonging to the moral sphere. In that we practice the spiritual 'technique' of moral growth in our souls, we bring about the penetration of the moral sphere into the growth in nature. *Rosicrucianism* is that stage of moral responsibility where we become conscious that within our inner life we bear a responsibility to the world, to nature—and in response we then begin to work on our inner life *in order that* it contributes to the healing of nature. One works to realize the 'Rose Cross' for the redemption of the plant kingdom, as one works to realize the 'Philosopher's Stone' for the redemption of the mineral world. The true Rosicrucians took such a decisive stand with regard to *nature*, not because they wished to introduce and bring forth the natural science of today, but because they were conscious of humanity's moral responsibility towards nature, which is to say they were true Rosicrucians

5

THE WORK ON THE
FUTURE REDEMPTION OF
THE ANIMAL KINGDOM

THE *first* DIFFICULTY the meditator encounters is the inclination of consciousness to wander about. This starts as soon as our consciousness is not occupied with the sense world or with ideas and thoughts stirred up by the sense world. When beginning to meditate, we have the experience that we owe the inner consistency and order of our thoughts and ideas to the order of things in the outer world. If we no longer hold on to the order impressed upon us through sense experience and abandon the lines on which our thoughts and ideas have been accustomed to move through experience, then either instability and disorder set in, or a state of mindless perplexity ensues. This simple experience can however lead to important insights in the direction of self-knowledge and also of knowledge of our responsibilities. It points to the fact that we human beings are indeed upright beings in our physical bearing, and beings endowed in our consciousness with the ability to survey and form judgments. But this is primarily due to the world of physical experience and to our inner organization; it is not exclusively due to our own inner *bearing*, for which we have only ourselves to thank. Our *organization* is such that we do not merge into our immediate surroundings. We can raise ourselves above and survey them, but the power of our own inner bearing becomes evident at the moment consciousness relinquishes the outer world and the impetus of its stimuli. Initially it shows itself to be inadequate. It is apparent that we possess, as a gift, an upright organization raising itself into the vertical. However, when the stimulus and supports from outside are missing, our resulting consciousness 'lays itself down'; that is, it goes over into the passivity of the horizontal. Initially, consciousness in our physical organization experiences itself as standing in the vertical; then as it passes over into the ether body it becomes horizontal. So also does ordinary thinking that has not been strengthened through meditation, and occurs principally in the ether body, pass into the horizontal. The physical eyebrows are the outer expression for the two horizontal ether currents that stream right and left in the ordinary thinking process. This thinking 'doubts' all that lies outside ordinary experience. It is itself always divided. The participation of one's own 'I' consists 'in creating the thinking 'axis of vision' in relation to what is provided by the right and left thought currents—that is, the 'I' only makes the *connection* between the Luciferic and Ahrimanic currents of thoughts and ideas. However, when questions are directed towards supersensible facts, where spiritual processes and beings are the concern, ordinary thinking is initially powerless to create this connection. The two currents of thoughts are not oriented for this— and therefore *doubt* arises. That is, the condition of consciousness where *two* opposing thought currents, unconnected and disunited, work against each other.

In order that the 'I' become master over doubt, what matters is not its partaking in the left or right current, but the bringing about of a *third* stream that no longer runs in the horizontal but takes place in the vertical. The effort to create this third kind of thought current is precisely that of *meditation*. The first and fundamental task of meditative exercises is to create a vertical thought current that streams from above downwards; that is, from the spiritual world into the physical.

If this current is created, then 'doubt' is overcome as an obstacle to knowledge of higher worlds. Doubt then remains only as an aid so that, in the realm of the physical world, form and maturity can be granted to what has become known in the vertical. A kind of thinking begins that presents a bridge into the spiritual world, and over this bridge regular communication between the two worlds may be cultivated. The presence of this kind of communication is, further, something that has a deep *moral* significance. For not only are far more intensive questions and answers activated through this discerning consciousness than is the case with ordinary thinking, but also the moral task to remain *loyal* to this relationship with the spiritual world is presented. The spiritual world is to the physical world as the world of becoming is to the world that has become. The spiritual world is the future, it bears within itself the positive future. Loyalty towards the spiritual world has therefore the moral implication of the duty *to remain loyal to the future.* This duty is something other than what one usually understands by loyalty, that is, loyalty towards the past. One is loyal, for example, if one relates to someone today in just the same way as one did many years ago; if one keeps a past alive and preserves it, one is loyal. But towards the spiritual world loyalty represents something else. Here it is being loyal to the *future* that counts. And one can only be loyal to the future by constantly striving to recognize and to realize the future, not by looking back on the past in order to preserve it. Therefore, if one remains stationary in particular forms of knowledge and in a particular type of activity, one becomes in this sense disloyal to the spiritual world. For then one abandons the way of the creative realization of the future; one becomes disloyal to the duty to be in constant change. The most important duty of the future towards the spiritual world consists in being indispensably engaged in change in order to seek and to find the ways from the great to the sublime, the true to the wisdom-filled, the good to the perfected.

The moral strength that loyalty to the future makes possible and that overcomes the doubt that experiences itself as powerless before opposition, was long ago designated as the power of *hope* (*elpis*). And *true* hope, as the result of the life of knowledge having been raised into the vertical, is what protects us from the danger of illness through imbalance, just as *faith* protects us from the danger of fixed idea, and *love* from the danger of apathy. There is also the danger that, filled with longing for the spiritual world in our sub-conscious soul-life, we pursue this longing by occupying ourselves with revelations from the spiritual world coming to us in one way or another. We cannot or will not bring ourselves to make those efforts that raise the current of thinking into the vertical. It can then happen that the more we receive spiritual values into ourselves, the stronger and more gnawing the doubt that grows within us. Doubting can ultimately develop into something immense; indeed, consciousness can as it were finally drown in a sea of doubt. And this path can lead to another pathological state: what was originally felt as inner comfort can become lack of courage in knowledge. This lack of courage in knowledge can then lead to a skepticism that, as its last stage, assumes the soul condition of despair now turned pathological. This is commonly termed 'black melancholy'.

Fixed ideas, dullness (apathy), and melancholy are the three spiritual diseases that threaten those who do not wish to make use of the means that can lead them to the spring of 'faith', 'love', and 'hope'. These are the three rays of the healing Christ-impulse. Just as faith, as a force, protects us from fixed ideas by way of the twelve fundamental outlooks of the world, corresponding to the twelve signs of the zodiac; just as love, in fullness of selfless interest for the moral spheres of space of the seven 'planets' rescues us from a threatening sense of dullness; so hope, as the capacity to let the *spiritual sun* rise up in our souls and remain there untarnished, rescues us from the danger of the 'inner solar eclipse' of black melancholy. More is meant by the 'inner sun' and 'inner solar eclipse' than a mere comparison for the sake of clarity; what we are concerned with here is a real spiritual fact—for hope is also a power that has to do with the cosmic, just as do faith and love. Just as what counts with faith and love is the spiritual regulation of the relationship to the zodiac and to the planetary spheres, so what counts with faith is the spiritual regulation of the relationship to *sun*, *earth*, and *moon*. We are in truth dealing now with a spiritual regulation of this relationship. When we abandon the firm ground of our physical organization and the earthly domain of experience, we face the task of not lapsing into the horizontal direction of what is moon-like; instead we must raise ourselves into the vertical as a ray of the spiritual sun. The upright stream of 'hope' is sun-like: it is the *inner* spiritual standing that must be learned through meditation, over and above the bodily physical standing.

Learning additional spiritually upright bearing, that is, true self-sufficiency, is an undertaking that, again, does not simply have subjective meaning for us ourselves but incorporates itself into spiritual-karmic world happenings. To first attain and then maintain the upright position of the spiritual-vertical in consciousness depends upon the overcoming of the *horizontal tendency* that is operative not only in our inner life but also outside us in nature. Indeed, it is operative in nature in the animal kingdom; it is the fate of the beings of this kingdom.

The power of the horizontal stream condemns animals to dumbness and to living by instinct alone. An upright bearing—as a working of 'heliotropism' on the organization of the human being—is necessary in order to be able to speak and think. Because it is totally absorbed in instinct, the animal is dumb. It cannot raise itself above instinct to be able to pass judgment and comment *upon* the instinct and the conditions surrounding it. It can never raise itself above these and attain an overview, but must 'swim along with' the currents driving it. The animal is compelled by the horizontal working of the moon to be in, and to stay in, the flow of that activity. This is the fate of animals. Thus constrained, they remain prisoners.

It is through the experience of the power of the horizontal current that human beings become aware in their inner life of another 'relationship between microcosm and macrocosm', that is, the great task of conscience to free the animal kingdom from the constraint of that power. The path we must tread to fulfill this task is that of creating in our inner life the transition from the moon-like to the sun-like. This transition is possible in that human thinking, which is initially moon-like, carries in itself precisely through this fact the possibility of being transformed into the sun-like. For just as the physical moon reflects the sunlight, so is ordinary thinking a reflection of that thinking which is actually the self-remembering below of that which is perceived above. But the light-filled, logical, and clear quality of ordinary thinking is still of sun-like origin. Hence the possibility arises for us to direct our thinking beyond the objects of ordinary thinking to their origin, that is to say to live in a thought not for its relationship to the outer world of experience (for its knowledge value) but in order to pass through the threshold of that thought into a conscious relationship with the sources from which it has flowed. This is the task of *meditation*: by means of a thought to arrive at the experience of the forces of which that thought is an inner reflection.

By such efforts consciousness is led from 'moon-like' thinking to 'sun-like' spirit-enlightened being, thereby working also through these efforts towards overcoming that power compelling the animal kingdom to dumbness. For it then connects itself with the spiritual Moon, the 'eye of the gods' (as Rudolf Steiner described it) through which spiritual sunlight can shine in. The light of the spiritual Sun-being thereby shines into the earthly sphere of existence and brings about the future overcoming of the fatal moon-magic for the kingdom of the animals. Just as the fixed-star constellations effect the numbness of the mineral kingdom and the planets the dullness of the plant world, so does the moon effect the constraint that holds sway over the animals. Through 'faith' we can make the spiritual forces of the zodiac active in earthly existence for the redemption of the mineral world; through 'love' we can radiate the spiritual forces of the planetary spheres in nature for the redemption of the plant kingdom; through 'hope' we can allow the Sun-being to work in through the gate of the spiritual Moon in order to free the animals from the constraint of the outer moon activity.

Rudolf Steiner describes this task of man's redemption of the animal kingdom in *An Outline of Esoteric Science*. There he speaks about the future task of humanity toward nature, and also toward the part of humanity that will remain behind:

In the course of its development, the good portion of humankind will learn to use the Moon forces to transform the evil part so that it can participate in further evolution as a distinct earthly kingdom. Through the work of the good part of humanity, the Earth, then reunited with the Moon, will become able to reunite with the Sun after a certain period of evolution, and also with the other planets. After an interim stage that resembles a sojourn in a higher world, the Earth will transform itself into the Jupiter state.

During the Jupiter stage, what is now called the mineral kingdom will not exist; mineral forces will have been transformed into plant forces. The lowest kingdom appearing during the Jupiter stage will be the plant kingdom, which will have a form entirely different from what it has now. Above that will be the animal kingdom which will have undergone a *transformation*, followed by a human kingdom consisting of the descendents of the evil union that came about on Earth. Above these, there will be a higher human kingdom consisting of the descendents of the community of good human beings on Earth.[1]

And indeed, the transformed animal kingdom is *transformed* inasmuch as it is freed from spiritual sunlessness through the efforts of the advanced part of humankind, while the lower human kingdom will consist of the descendants of those human beings who have rejected 'faith', 'love', and 'hope' and have thereby karmically fallen victim to one-sidedness, to apathy, and to melancholy.

Work on the Foundation Stone is fundamental to beginning the task of freeing the animal kingdom, not simply because it is a *meditation* (for in a certain sense *every* meditative effort is such a beginning), but because it also contains in its four verses the spiritual forces of redemption of the archetypal beings of the animal kingdom. Thus the *first* verse of the Foundation Stone is the verse that carries the force of redemption for those animals representative of 'metabolism'.[2] The *second* verse relates to those animal beings who have their characteristic attribute in the 'breast system'.[3] The *third* verse has significance for the part of the animal kingdom that has found its origin in the one-sided forming of the 'head organization'.[4] The *fourth* verse, however, relates to the part of humankind that now stands in danger of gradually losing its humanity, allowing a future animal/human kingdom to arise.[5]

The significance of the Foundation Stone for the animal kingdom is that the verses allow the primeval picture of the 'bull', the 'lion', the 'eagle', and the 'human being' to arise from the depths. This picture is understood in the sense of the duties and tasks of conscience, as we have tried to characterize above. This, together

1. Op. cit., page 393. Italics added by Valentin Tomberg.
2. Traditionally represented by the 'bull'.
3. Traditionally represented by the 'lion'.
4. Traditionally represented by the 'eagle'.
5. On this account the fourth verse is directed to Christ, who is the bearer of the true 'I' according to the words of St. Paul: 'Not I, but Christ in me.'

with the Rose-Cross and the Stone in the form of the dodecahe-dron, produce the three levels of penetration into the depths of the Foundation Stone from the point of view of the 'relationship between microcosm and macrocosm.' These are the tasks we have toward nature, and with which we have been entrusted.

FURTHER READING

Collected early articles and essays written by Valentin Tomberg are scheduled to be published in the year 2010 by LogoSophia Press under the title *Russian Spirituality and Other Essays: Mysteries of Our Time Seen Through the Eyes of a Russian Esotericist*. These articles, spanning the years 1930–1938, deal in great depth with the spiritual life of Eastern Europe and Russia, themes from early Christianity, and the relationship of these to the anthroposophical understanding of the human being. The text is a revised translation (with some articles added and some omitted) of *Early Articles: Spiritual Science and the World Situation*, first published in 1984.

Christ and Sophia: Anthroposophic Meditations on the Old Testament, New Testament, and Apocalypse (Gt. Barrington, MA: SteinerBooks, 2006). *Christ and Sophia* contains all of Valentin Tomberg's essential anthroposophic works on the Scriptures, providing an invaluable resource for anyone who wishes to gain a deeper understanding of esoteric Christianity, as revealed by a close, meditative reading of the Bible—from *Genesis* to John's *Revelation*. The appendix contains his seven lectures held in Rotterdam in 1939 entitled *The Four Sacrifices of Christ and the Reappearance of Christ in the Etheric World*.

Inner Development, 7 lectures held in Rotterdam in 1938 (Gt. Barrington, MA: Anthroposophic Press, 1992). These talks deal with the spiritual path in its Christian-Rosicrucian aspect, discussing the deeper significance of meditation, the various stages of consciousness (Imagination, Inspiration, and Intuition), the Guardian of the Threshold, and the esoteric trials one encounters along the way, concluding with a description of the life of Rudolf Steiner as the life of a Christian initiate.

Lazarus, Come Forth! Meditations of a Christian Esotericist on the Mysteries of the Raising of Lazarus, the Ten Commandments, the

Three Kingdoms & the Breath of Life (Gt. Barrington, MA: Lindis-farne Books, 2006). Drawing on the ancient and often-forgotten sources of esoteric Christianity, Valentin Tomberg reflects on the mysteries of humanity's covenant with God in history. The power of these meditations is that they reflect the author's personal spiritual journey into the depths of God's kingdom within—within the soul, within personal relationships, within nature and the cosmos. A pre-vious edition of this work was titled *Covenant of the Heart.*

Meditations on the Tarot: A Journey into Christian Hermeticism (New York: Putnam/Jeremy P. Tarcher, 2002). This book is one of the true spiritual classics of the twentieth century. Published with an index and Cardinal Hans Urs von Balthasar's Afterword, this publication is one of the most important works of esoteric Chris-tianity. Written anonymously and published posthumously, as was the author's wish, the intention of this work is for the reader to find a relationship with the author in the spiritual dimensions of exist-ence. The author wanted not to be thought of as a personality who lived from 1900 to 1973, but as a friend who is communicating with us from beyond the boundaries of ordinary life. *Meditations on the Tarot* is a timely contribution toward the rediscovery and renewal of the Christian contemplative tradition of the Fathers of the Church and the High Middle Ages.

The Wandering Fool: Love & Its Symbols. Early Studies on the Tarot, with Three Lectures on Christian Hermeticism by Robert Powell (San Rafael, CA: LogoSophia Press, 2009). Students of *Meditations on the Tarot* have cause for celebration, for in 2007 a collection of the author's notes was published—preliminary studies of the images of the Tarot cards, illustrating the method he followed This method-ology is now revealed for the first time in English translation through the inclusion of material published in Part Two of this volume. Part One comprises three lectures held by Robert Powell, the translator of *Meditations on the Tarot* into English from the original French manuscript. Also included is additional background material from the Luxembourg (Kairos) and German (Achamoth) editions.

The Foundation Stone Meditation in the Sacred Dance of Eurythmy, by Lacquanna Paul and Robert Powell (study material published by the Sophia Foundation of North America).

Printed in Great Britain
by Amazon

47881052R00061